well preserved

well preserved

pickles, relishes, jams and chutneys for the new cook

Mary Anne Dragan

Whitecap Books
Vancouver/Toronto

The information in this book is true and complete to the best of our knowledge. All recommendations are made without guarantee on the part of the author or Whitecap Books. The author and publisher disclaim any liability in connection with the use of this information. For additional information, please contact Whitecap Books, 351 Lynn Avenue, North Vancouver, BC V7J 2C4.

Edited by Elaine Jones
Proofread by Elizabeth McLean
Cover and interior design by Antonia Banyard
Cover photographs by Lionel Trudel
Interior photographs by Lionel Trudel
Food styling by Nathan Fong

Printed and bound in Canada by Friesens, Altona, Manitoba.

Canadian Cataloguing in Publication Data
Dragan, Mary Anne, 1959–
  Well preserved

  Includes index.
  ISBN 1-55110-766-X

  1. Canning and preserving.   I. Title.
TX601.D72 1998   641.8'52   C98-910655-1

The publisher acknowledges the support of the Canada Council for the Arts and the Cultural Services Branch of the Government of British Columbia for our publishing program. We acknowledge the financial support of the Government of Canada through the Book Industry Development Program for our publishing activities.

Contents

Introduction

When I was a child growing up in Nova Scotia, everyone's mom did some kind of home canning. It always seemed to be a rather old-fashioned, out-dated activity, at least as far as we kids were concerned. We couldn't understand why anyone would want to spend long, hot hours working in the kitchen, in the middle of the summer, when jams and pickles could be had at any grocery store.

Now I wonder why anyone would prefer a store-bought product, when it is so easy and so much fun to make delicious preserves at home. For the price of a basket of produce and an hour or two of your time, you can enjoy the exceptional taste and quality of a homemade jam, pickle, chutney or relish year-round, and savor the knowledge that you made it yourself.

Preserves are easier to make than you think. If you like cooking, you're going to love home preserving. There's a back-to-nature, homey goodness about it that makes it a very satisfying pastime. And provided that you follow some simple, basic techniques and observe the guidelines for selecting and preparing produce, proper hygiene and careful storage, preserving will be a successful and rewarding experience.

For a time, home preserving had become something of a lost art, but it is now enjoying a vigorous revival. The desire for excellent food without unnecessary preservatives has greatly contributed to its renewed popularity. Gardening and the preservation of home-grown produce have become a way of life for more and more people.

Food preservation is no longer the tedious, time-consuming activity of Grandmother's day. Thanks to modern equipment and innovations, preparation and cooking times have been dramatically reduced. Techniques are continually being refined so that foods can be safely preserved and still retain flavor, color, texture and nutrients. Although there are countless varieties of store-bought preserves to choose from, none can compare with the vibrant, glorious flavors of the ones you make yourself.

Homemade preserves generally contain less sugar and salt than their commercially produced counterparts, and because they contain no artificial additives designed to prolong shelf life, homemade preserves are usually more wholesome as well. You know exactly what is inside the jar because you put it there yourself. If you choose, you can make healthful, delicious preserves using organically grown fruits and vegetables.

Fat-free relishes and salsas allow you to enhance otherwise bland dishes and may take the place of rich sauces. Select only the freshest fruits and vegetables, and the best available ingredients for your preserves, as preserving cannot improve the quality of food, it simply maintains it. If only the best goes into the jar, you will have a truly superior final product.

Food preservation makes sense economically too. Homemade tastes twice as good as store-bought and costs about half as much. You can even create luxurious specialty items at a fraction of what they would cost at an upscale grocery store, while taking advantage of the abundance of fruits and vegetables in your summer garden or local farmer's market.

The art of preserving brings us closer to nature — we

become more in tune with the passage of the seasons, it encourages us to use up and recycle, and it places an emphasis on fresh, natural ingredients preserved for future use at their peak of perfection.

Not least, preserving is fun. There is plenty of room for imagination in home preserving, so after you have gained some confidence, experiment a little with your own inventive combinations of fruits, vegetables, herbs and spices. Who knows? You could be creating a favorite family recipe that will be cherished and handed down by future generations.

This book is designed to give you just a taste of preserving — to whet your appetite for it. All the preserves in this book can be safely canned at home with a minimum of equipment in a reasonable period of time. You will learn how to make several types of sweet preserves: jams and jellies and their relatives, marmalades, conserves, preserves, fruit sauces and butters. The next section covers savory condiments, such as pickles, relishes, chutneys and ketchups. There is a chapter on infusing vinegars with fresh fruit and herbs, and another with ideas on how to use your homemade preserves in a variety of mouth-watering recipes. The last chapter offers suggestions on how to give your preserves as gifts and ideas for creatively packaging and decorating them.

If you've never tried it, give home preserving a chance. By following the rules you can produce consistently excellent preserves with little time and effort. Your reward will be cupboards filled with mouth-watering condiments to complement every meal, and the satisfaction of rows of gleaming jars adorning your pantry shelves.

The Basics
of Preserving

What Is Preserving?

Preserving food means to store and protect it from spoilage so that it can be eaten safely at some time in the future. There are many methods of food preservation; some, like drying, date back to prehistoric times. Other methods of food preservation include fermenting, brining, salting and smoking. This book covers the preservation of foods in vacuum-sealed glass jars, a procedure known as preserving, or canning. The term canning sometimes causes confusion to those who are unfamiliar with it, since cans are not actually involved. In the past, some cooks did preserve food at home in cans, but today this is virtually unheard-of.

Canning is generally understood to mean the process of preparing foods in airtight jars. It is one of the most reliable methods for preserving foods. In the 19th century, Nicolas Appert, a native of France, developed canning in response to Napoleon's request for a way to preserve foods for his troops. Appert's efforts laid the groundwork for modern canning. Not long afterwards, Louis Pasteur proved that food spoilage is caused by microorganisms present in air, water and soil. His discoveries led to further developments in preserving methods and equipment. Even today, methods for canning or preserving are constantly being reviewed and improved.

Why Does Food Spoil?

All food preservation methods are based on simple principles. To preserve foods safely and effectively, we must control enzymes and microorganisms naturally occurring in foods that can cause them to spoil. Containers of preserved food must also be thoroughly sealed to prevent the reintroduction of air-borne microorganisms and to counteract oxidation.

Enzymes are organic substances in foods. They are absolutely essential for fruits and vegetables to ripen, but if left unchecked, the action of enzymes will ultimately cause food to spoil. For this reason, it is advisable to process fresh produce as soon as possible after picking. Enzymatic action is destroyed by heat. Heat is also the easiest and most effective way to kill microorganisms. Most molds, yeasts and bacteria are killed at the temperature of boiling water. Most, but not all...

A dangerous bacterium, *Clostridium botulinum*, can form spores able to withstand extremely high temperatures. While heat will kill the bacteria, it encourages the formation of spores that, given the right conditions, can later germinate. Coincidentally, the conditions necessary for the spores to flourish and grow are exactly those that exist inside a jar of canned food: the absence of air and a moist environment. These bacteria produce a poisonous toxin that causes the deadly disease botulism.

C. botulinum cannot grow in the presence of acid, so high-acid foods such as fruits and other foods preserved with vinegar or lemon juice will prevent its growth, providing proper canning procedures are followed.

There are only two widely accepted methods for processing canned foods: the boiling water bath method and pressure canning. Both procedures use heat to destroy microorganisms and inactivate enzymes. Pressure canning is reserved for low-acid foods such as meat, poultry, fish or vegetables preserved without vinegar. The extended time and higher temperatures used in this procedure will destroy spores and bacteria not normally eliminated at the temperature of boiling water. Pressure canning requires specialized equipment—a pressure canner is a considerable investment.

All the preserves in this book may be safely processed using the boiling water bath method, as they contain sufficient acid to prevent the growth of bacteria.

How Does Preserving Actually Work?

Preserving arrests the spoilage of fresh food by heating it in a sealed container. The food is prepared and placed in hot, sterilized jars. It is then heated in the jars to a temperature sufficient to destroy spoilage agents. During the heating process, air remaining in the food and in the space at the top of the jar is driven out between the jar and the special canning jar lid.

As the jar and the contents cool, the vacuum that has been created inside the jar sucks the lid inward, holding it tightly in place until the jar is opened. This airtight seal prevents any further contamination unless the seal is broken. This allows preserves to maintain their flavor and quality for a long time without refrigeration.

It is certainly possible to make virtually any type of preserve without heat processing. Such unprocessed preserves must be kept refrigerated and used within a short period of time.

Preserving Equipment

Using the right equipment will make preserving easier, safer and more successful. Only a few basic utensils are required for small-scale preserving. Fortunately, most of you will already have everything that you need in your own kitchens. There are also some specially designed, inexpensive tools that will save time and frustration, making your experience a more pleasurable one. These are optional, but recommended. And if you really get into preserving, there are additional time-saving gadgets that you will long to have.

The Preserving Pot

Without a doubt the most important piece of equipment is the preserving pot. It should be a wide, heavy pot with a thick bottom that will distribute heat evenly. A lightweight stock pot, for example, will *not* do. The even distribution of heat will help prevent scorching in foods that contain a lot of sugar. Straight-sided pots are best — they are especially useful for measuring the depth of liquid when a recipe calls for boiling a mixture until its volume is reduced by half.

The pot must be large enough to allow foods to bubble up the sides without overflowing. Some fruit and sugar mixtures expand considerably during rapid boiling — the juice and foam can rise amazingly high (alarmingly high if your pot is too small). Believe me, it is no picnic cleaning boiled-over jam or jelly off the top of your stove. A wide-diameter pot also speeds evaporation and reduces cooking time. A pot that is about three times the volume of your food is ideal. Eight to ten quarts (8 to 10 L) is a good all-purpose size.

Stainless steel or enamel-lined cast-iron pots are your best bets for preserving. Unlined cast-iron, copper, aluminum or galvanized pots will react with acids that are naturally present in foods, resulting in unpleasant flavors and colors.

Other Essentials
- ► measuring cups (liquid and dry)
- ► measuring spoons
- ► a stiff vegetable brush
- ► a selection of knives, including a sharp paring knife and a good, sturdy knife for chopping
- ► a cutting board
- ► a vegetable peeler
- ► a grater
- ► a citrus reamer or juicer
- ► a long-handled spoon for stirring, preferably with a metal bowl
- ► a slotted spoon
- ► a ladle
- ► a potato masher

- ▸ rubber spatulas
- ▸ tongs
- ▸ mixing bowls
- ▸ a colander, sieve, or both
- ▸ cheesecloth
- ▸ a timer
- ▸ hot pads or oven mitts
- ▸ rubber gloves
- ▸ jars, lids and screwbands (more on these below)
- ▸ a water-bath canner

Optional But Highly Recommended Tools
- ▸ a canning jar funnel (to fill jars without spilling)
- ▸ a jar lifter (to raise or lower jars into the boiling water bath)
- ▸ a jelly bag (to strain fruit pulp when making jelly)
- ▸ a candy thermometer (to determine when sweet preserves are sufficiently cooked)
- ▸ a food processor
- ▸ kitchen scales
- ▸ a citrus zester

Extras
- ▸ cake racks for cooling jars
- ▸ a cherry pitter
- ▸ a berry huller
- ▸ a food mill
- ▸ a magnetic lid lifter (for removing jar lids from hot water)
- ▸ a metal steamer or basket (for blanching tomatoes and peaches)

Canning Jars

Often called Mason jars after the inventive American John Mason, who pioneered their design, canning jars are now marketed under various brand names. Poor Mr. Mason apparently let his patent lapse, and other entrepreneurs were quick to jump on the bandwagon.

A complete box of canning jars will include the jars and a corresponding number of two-piece metal lids. These lids consist of a flat metal disc and a metal screwband (sometimes referred to as a ring). The underside of the disc is coated with an enamel that resists food acids. Take care not to scratch the discs to help prevent rusting. The edge of the disc is lined with a rubber sealing compound which softens slightly when heated and covers the rim of the jar to form a seal. The metal screwband holds the disc in place and should be firmly tightened. During heat processing, the two-piece lid allows heat to escape, releasing pressure that builds up inside the jar.

Each time you make preserves, check your jars to ensure that they are not chipped or cracked. Check new jars, too, just to be sure. Wash all jars in hot, soapy water and carefully sterilize them before each use.

A box of canning jars contains one other thing: excellent instructions that explain how to safely and successfully use them. Follow these instructions.

Canning jars are made with two sizes of openings: standard mouth (2⅜ inches/6 cm) and wide mouth (3 inches/7.5 cm). You may come across a third size, the gem or jewel jar, which has an opening that falls somewhere in between. These jars are no longer being manufactured, but lids and screwbands are available for purchase to accommodate people who may still have these jars at home.

Jars are available in various sizes (capacities):

½ cup (4 oz.)	125 mL
½ pint (8 oz.)	250 mL (236 mL)
pint (16 oz.)	500 mL
quart (32 oz.)	1 litre
2 quart (64 oz.)	2 litre

The half-pint, pint and quart are most commonly used. The half-cup (125-mL) size is so tiny, I find it suitable only for gifts, when I want to give a variety of preserves in small, taster sizes.

The half-pint (250 mL) is an excellent size for jams and jellies. It may appear as 236 mL just to make things confusing, but you may use the 250-mL and 236-mL sizes interchangeably.

The two-quart (2-L) size is not recommended. First, it is almost impossible to find a pot deep enough to handle jars this size. Second, it takes so long for heat to penetrate the food at the center of the jar that the process would take far too long. Besides, who needs that much food in one jar? So do yourself a favor and stick to the more common sizes.

Select the size of jar and the diameter of the mouth according to the type of food that you are preserving. Another consideration is the size of your family. There is no point putting up jam in teensy-weensy jars if you have four teenage children.

Through experience, I have found that certain jars accommodate particular types of foods best. For each recipe, I have indicated the size of jar that I feel is most appropriate.

Liquid-type foods, such as jams, jellies, marmalades and ketchups, that pour easily when hot are best in regular-mouth jars. The narrow opening decreases the likelihood of splashing. For most people, the half-pint (250-mL) jars are most practical for sweet spreads, but pints may also be used.

Chunky or thick foods do best in wide-mouth jars as it is

easier to ladle the preserves into a larger opening. Relishes, chutneys and butters are included in this group. Either a half-pint (250-mL) or a pint (500-mL) jar may be suitable. A half-pint, wide-mouth jar is generally sold as a jar for canning salmon, but these are perfect for small sizes of relish and chutney. Wide-mouth jars are also best for foods that need to be individually arranged inside the jars, such as some types of pickles. Quart (litre) jars are recommended for large or long vegetables, such as whole cucumbers, beans or asparagus.

Canning jars are made of sturdy tempered glass designed to withstand high temperatures. Do not be tempted to recycle regular commercial jars. Using old mayonnaise or peanut butter jars may seem like a money-saving idea, but they are made from a lighter-weight glass that may shatter during filling or heat processing. Jars which are not specifically designed for canning also may not seal properly. Considering the time and effort you will spend on preserving, it is not worth risking accidents or food spoilage by using such jars.

A supply of canning jars may seem rather expensive initially, but remember, they are recyclable. If you handle and store your jars carefully, you will be able to use them year after year. As long as they are in perfect condition, the jars and metal screwbands may be used time and time again, but the lids are designed for single use only. They will not seal properly if used a second time; throw them away once used. Replacement lids are available at a minimal cost. You must also discard screwbands that are bent or rusty. Nifty one-piece, screw-on plastic caps are available for refrigerator storage of your preserves. These are much more convenient than dealing with lids and screwbands every time you want to open up a jar. They are available in grocery stores and most places that sell canning jars.

Buy your canning jars early in the spring or summer to

ensure a good supply later on in the year. Many stores only carry jars during what they consider to be "the canning season" and they do not restock jars once they sell out, for fear of having to carry them over the winter. You may find it difficult to track down jars by mid-August.

Shop around for jars, as prices vary widely from place to place. Keep an eye open for sales. Garage sales, secondhand stores and rummage sales are good sources for reasonably priced jars, but you will usually need to buy new lids and screwbands. Once your friends discover that you are preserving, you will be showered with secondhand jars. (Could they have ulterior motives?) Some of these may be suitable. Always examine recycled jars very carefully to be sure they are not damaged.

The Preserving Process

How to Sterilize Jars

- Wash the jars (including new jars) in hot, soapy water and dry thoroughly. Or simply run them through the regular cycle of your dishwasher.

- Place the clean jars in a large pot. You can use the same pot you will be using for the water bath.

- Cover the jars with water and bring to a boil.

- Boil the jars for 15 minutes.

- Turn off the heat, cover the pot and keep the jars hot until you are ready to fill them.

Preparing the Jar Lids

Only the jar lids, not the metal screwbands, need advance preparation.

The rubber compound on the inside of the lid needs to be softened so it will adhere to the rim of the jar and seal the jar properly. Heating the lids in boiling water sterilizes the lids and also softens the rubber compound.

- ▶ Bring a small pot of water to a boil.
- ▶ Place the jar lids inside the pot and simmer over low heat for 15 minutes.
- ▶ Cover the pot and keep the lids hot until you are ready to use them.

    It is not a good idea to boil the lids for long periods of time.

- ▶ Use tongs to remove the lids from the hot water as you need them. (A magnetic wand specially designed for this very purpose is available from canning-jar manufacturers.)

What Is Head Space?

When preserving food in jars, never fill the jars right to the rim. The space between the contents of the jar and the lid is known as the head space.

Head space allows room for expansion of the food during heat processing. It should be just enough to permit food to swell as it is heated without danger of it overflowing, but not so much that an excess of air would prevent a good vacuum seal from being formed.

Food that escapes the jar during heat processing does far more damage than just causing a big mess. Particles of food on the rims or threads of a jar can interfere with a perfect seal, and can contribute to the growth of mold. Mold on the outside of a jar will eventually force its way under the lid and ruin the seal, causing the food inside to spoil.

If you leave too large a head space, the air inside the jar may prevent a proper seal from forming. Excess air may also cause foods to discolor due to oxidation.

Most preserves require about a ½-inch (1.2-cm) head space, but density, shape and particular characteristics of foods can all affect head space specifications.

Because steam expands more at higher altitudes, those who live at altitudes in excess of 1000 feet (300 m) above sea level must leave a bit more head space inside the jars. Allow an extra ⅛ inch (.3 cm) for every 1000 feet (300 m) above sea level.

Releasing Air Bubbles

Sometimes air is trapped between the food and the jar as the food is placed inside during packing. Air bubbles (pockets of air) can prevent liquid from completely covering or surrounding the food, and may contribute to food spoiling. Air bubbles are more likely to happen with some types of foods than with others. Relishes and pickled vegetables and fruits are particular culprits.

After the jars are packed, run a thin non-metal object, such as a plastic knife or spatula, around the inside of each jar, between the food and the glass. This will dislodge the bubbles. Do not use a metal knife or any sharp utensil which could make tiny scratches or nicks in the glass. The high temperatures during heat processing stress the glass and may cause it to break along these weakened spots.

If additional space is created at the top of the jar after the air bubbles have been released, add more liquid to the jar to return it to the proper level before closing it. The correct head space helps to create a good vacuum seal.

If you don't dislodge air bubbles, you may find that once the food cools and the liquid settles, there will be extra space at the top of the jar between the food and the lid. Certain foods, like pickles, may end up protruding above the level of the liquid. This is unattractive and foods at the top of the jar will soon discolor. It is best to refrigerate such jars and use the preserves as soon as possible.

The Boiling Water Bath

Unless they are to be kept refrigerated, all preserves must be processed in a boiling water bath. Many people believe that it is not necessary to heat process certain types of preserves, such as jams or jellies, but experts agree that this additional step must be taken to ensure that homemade preserves are safe to eat.

Despite your most scrupulous efforts at cleanliness, bacteria, molds and spores may be present in the foods you are preserving. Airborne microorganisms may also contaminate foods as they are being placed into jars.

Heat processing in a boiling water bath will destroy any microorganisms that may be lurking in your homemade preserves. For safety's sake, do not omit this vital procedure.

Any large pot will do for a water bath canner provided that it meets certain requirements.

The pot must be deep enough to allow at least 2 inches (5 cm) of water to cover the jars when they are placed inside, as well as permitting sufficient space for boiling. A pot about 10 inches (25 cm) deep is good for pints (500 mL); allow about 12 inches (30 cm) for quart (1-L) jars.

The pot must be large enough to hold several jars at a time so that they are not touching one another, allowing the water to circulate freely around them. (Jars that are packed in too tightly could crack as they expand with the heat.)

There should be room at the bottom of the pot for a metal rack, such as a cake rack, to elevate the jars slightly. [You can improvise a rack for elevating jars by tying several old canning rings (screwbands) together and placing them right side up inside the bottom of the pot.] The pot should be no more than 4 inches (10 cm) greater in diameter than the burner that you will be using. And finally, your canner must have a snug-fitting lid.

Of course, there are pots specifically designed for water

bath canning. These large deep pots, usually made from enamel-coated metal or stainless steel, come equipped with a specially fitted, basket-shaped rack to hold your jars of preserves in place and have high or folding handles that enable you to lift the entire rack full of jars from the boiling water. A genuine water bath canner is an excellent investment if you plan to do a lot of preserving.

Precisely when you prepare the boiling water bath depends on how long it will take to make your preserves. There is no point having the water boiling merrily away while foods are being washed or chopped up, for example, or if they have to be steeped or soaked for a lengthy period.

The boiling water bath should be ready to go as soon as your jars are filled, so that the hot jars can immediately be placed in the pot and the heat processing can begin.

If you are using the same pot that you used to sterilize the jars, then it is very easy. After all the jars have been filled and any extras removed from the pot, simply turn the heat to high,

Adjustments for Altitude

Altitude affects certain aspects of preserving. Water boils at a lower temperature at higher altitudes, due to decreased atmospheric pressure. This affects two preserving operations: testing for the gel stage using a thermometer and processing preserves in a boiling water bath.

Testing for the gel stage: At elevations up to 1000 feet (300 m), the gel stage for preserves is reached at 220°F (104°C). Temperatures that refer to the gel stage in this book are for such elevations.

To determine the gel stage at elevations above 1000 feet (300 m), add 8°F (4°C) to the boiling point of water at your elevation.

The boiling water bath: At altitudes of 1000 feet (300 m) and above, the processing time in a boiling water bath will be longer.

For preserves that are normally processed for 20 minutes or less (all of the preserves in this book), add 1 minute extra processing time for each additional 1000 feet (300 m) above sea level.

cover the pot and bring the water to a boil. Since the water is already hot, this won't take long.

The jars will displace the water as they are put in the pot, causing the water level to rise considerably. There is usually enough water in the canner to cover the jars sufficiently. However, it is convenient to have an extra pot of hot water simmering just in case you need to add some. You don't want to have to start boiling cold water at this stage.

If your canner has a basket, fill it with the jars and lower it carefully into the water. If you are using a regular pot, place the jars inside, one by one, onto the rack in the bottom of the pot, standing them upright so that none of them are touching any others. It is very helpful to have a proper jar lifter for this, so that you don't scald your hands with the boiling water. If you don't have a jar lifter, wear rubber gloves to protect your hands. For small jam-sized jars, you can use regular tongs to grasp the tops of the jars and then place them in the canner. Larger jars will have to be placed in by hand. If you are performing this tricky operation, don't fill the canner as full at the outset, but do have the extra pot of hot water standing by. The lower level of water in the canner will allow you to safely put the jars into the pot without burning yourself. Top up the water to cover the jars using the water in the smaller pot. Whew! This is sounding a lot more complicated than it really is.

Once the jars are in the canner, cover it and let the water return to a boil. Start timing from the moment the water starts to boil again. Lower the heat a bit if necessary to keep the water from overflowing, but make sure that the water remains at a steady boil.

When the time is up, remove the jars and place them on a wire rack or a heat-proof surface to cool. Allow enough space for air to circulate freely around the jars. Never place the jars on a cold surface — they could crack.

How to Know When Jars Are Sealed

► You can hear it. As they cool, most jar lids will make a popping sound—music to the ears of home preservers! If you tap the lid with a spoon, a clear ringing sound indicates the seal is complete.

► You can see it. If you hold the jar at eye level, you can see a slight indentation in the center of the lid (the surface is concave). A flat or bulging lid is not sealed.

► You can feel it. Push down on the center of the lid with your finger. A properly sealed jar will not respond to pressure on its lid. If the lid gives then pops back up when your finger is removed, the jar is not sealed.

A final way to check for properly sealed jars is to remove the screwband. If the lids are sealed, you can lift the jar by the lid.

Be patient. Give the jars a chance to seal. Some take up to 24 hours.

You do not need to perform all of these tests to be certain that your jars are sealed. They are included more for reassurance than anything else. The fingertip pressure test is adequate.

Occasionally, a jar will appear to have sealed, then later on the lid will pop back up again. For this reason, it's a good idea to check jars once they have cooled and once again before you use the preserves.

Reprocessing unsealed jars is not recommended. Refrigerate unsealed jars and use them as soon as possible.

Storing Your Preserves

Storing preserved foods, even in a small city apartment, is not a big problem. Foods that are preserved in jars have an advantage over frozen foods in that preserves require no special equipment to keep them. While not all of us are fortunate enough to have a separate, temperature-controlled pantry or root cellar, most homes have several places that are suitable for keeping preserves.

Cool, dark and dry—these are the words to remember when storing your preserves.

▸ Ideally, the temperature should be 40° to 50°F (5° to 10°C), but this is not always possible. Even properly processed foods will lose vitamins and nutrients above 50°F (10°C) and if the temperature is high enough, certain types of bacteria can reactivate and begin to grow inside the jars. Keep preserves away from extra warm areas near furnaces, fireplaces, heating pipes and vents.

Guard preserves from freezing. Freezing will not cause spoilage, but since foods expand as they freeze, the seals could be damaged or the jars could break. If the cool place that you have in mind is subject to freezing, wrap the jars in newspapers or blankets to insulate them.

▸ Light also destroys vitamins and can cause certain types of preserves to fade or darken unappetizingly. As attractive as they are, your preserves must be stored out of sight, away from the light.

▸ A dry storage area is crucial. Dampness or humidity can cause metal jar lids to rust.

▸ Arrange preserves in such a way that you can have good "stock rotation," using up the older foods before the newer ones. Well-made preserves should remain in good condition even after the next season comes along, provided they have been stored properly. After prolonged storage, however, flavor and quality will definitely suffer — it is not recommended to keep homemade preserves longer than one year — six months is best. If you find that you still have jars of one thing or another once the new season has arrived, make a mental note to prepare less of that particular item the next time.

- Don't forget to label your preserves. You may be able to tell the difference now, but six months later blueberry jam and blackberry jam will look exactly alike. And it's not always easy to tell which pickles are the mild ones and which are extra hot.

- Always check your jars for any signs of spoilage before using the preserves. Discard any jars that are even remotely questionable.

Basic Steps for Successful Preserving

- Read the recipe carefully.

- Check that you have all the ingredients and equipment you need before you start.

- Select the correct size and type of jars, ensuring that they are not chipped or cracked.

About Microwave Preserving

If you enjoy microwave cooking in general, you may want to try processing foods using the microwave.

The microwave can be used for making small amounts of preserves, but they will require very frequent stirring to prevent sticking or scorching, especially towards the end of the cooking time.

The most success is likely with very small batches using a maximum of 1 to 2 cups (240 to 475 mL) of fruit. Larger quantities tend to boil over.

I have found that it is more trouble to constantly open and close the door of the microwave than it is to stir a pot on top of the stove. And unless you are going to store your microwave preserves in the refrigerator, you must still sterilize your jars and process your preserves in boiling water—so you're using the stove anyway.

Consult a microwave cookbook for more information on microwave preserving.

- Wash the jars thoroughly, then sterilize the jars and lids and keep them hot until you are ready to use them.

- Prepare the water bath canner.

- Place the prepared preserves into the hot jars as directed in the recipe. Work quickly so that everything remains hot. Leave the recommended head space.

- Release air bubbles if necessary.

- Carefully wipe the rims of the jars free of any spilled food.

- Place the lids on the jars, rubber side down, and screw on the rings (screwbands) firmly, but not overly tight.

- Transfer the jars to the boiling water bath.

- Simmer the jars for the amount of time indicated in the recipe. Start timing once the water has returned to a boil.

- Remove the jars and place them on a heat-proof surface to cool.

- Cool the preserves for several hours or overnight.

- Once the jars have cooled, test for a seal. Refrigerate any jars that have not sealed properly.

- Remove the screwbands and wipe jars carefully with a damp cloth.

- Label the jars clearly, indicating the type of preserve and the date.

- Store preserves in a cool, dark, dry place.

Jams

Jam is so simple to make that perhaps the expression "as easy as pie" should be revised to "as easy a jam." (I don't know about you, but I find pie-making to be a rather daunting task!)

Easy, economical and satisfying to make, you can whip up a batch of homemade jam in as little as one hour from start to finish, although some recipes take a little longer. Making jam requires no special equipment—everything you need is already in your kitchen.

The taste of fresh fruit shines through homemade jam, unmasked by the excessive amounts of sugar and preservatives found in commercial products. You will find that the jams you make yourself have a slightly different texture than store-bought jams. Homemade jams tend to be of a softer consistency, set but not solid.

The beauty of jam is that there is a certain amount of room for error, if it doesn't thicken as much as you would like—it still tastes terrific.

Unlike some other types of preserves that take time to mature, jam is ready to eat as soon as you make it. But don't limit your enjoyment of jam to breakfast—jam can enhance many types of desserts. It makes an excellent filling for bars and cookies, or it can be sandwiched between the layers of a rich, homemade cake. (Try raspberry jam with chocolate cake.) Fill small tart shells with custard and a dollop of jam, then top

About Paraffin Wax

Many old recipes call for sealing jars of preserves using melted paraffin wax. Doubtless a great number of seasoned home preservers still seal jams and jellies using this method, but wax seals are no longer recommended as they do not always provide an airtight seal. As the wax cools, it can pull away from the sides of the jar, exposing the surface of the preserves to air. Tiny bubbles in the wax may open, creating holes through which air and microorganisms can enter, allowing mold to develop.

with fresh fruit; or thin jams with juice or alcohol to make marvelous, instant fruit sauces. A bit of jam added to plain, non-fat yogurt gives a boost of flavor and sweetness without too many extra calories. A spoonful of jam has about half as many calories as the same amount of butter; use jam instead of butter if you are watching your weight.

So delight your family and friends — simmer up a pot of old-fashioned, homemade jam. Your kitchen will be filled with mouth-watering aromas and visions of sweet surprises to come. What a treat it will be to enjoy a luscious, fresh-testing jam, made from the finest of juicy summer fruits, on a cold wintry morning in January. That is, if it lasts that long!

The Essentials of Making Jam

Jam is essentially just a mixture of mashed-up fruit and sugar, cooked together until thickened. The basic principle of making jam is to have a proper balance of fruit, sugar, pectin and acid. This will ensure a good set, meaning the jam will be soft enough to spread, but firm enough not to run off your toast.

Fruit: As in all preserving, it is crucial to use only the freshest, top-quality produce. The ideal is a mixture of ripe and slightly underripe fruit, as underripe fruit contains more natural pectin, critical in helping the jam to set. A good ratio is ¾ ripe fruit to ¼ slightly underripe, but not green, fruit. Never use overripe or mushy fruit. Wash the fruit carefully, even if it is to be peeled.

Sugar: The correct amount of sugar is necessary for a jam to thicken properly. Sugar acts as a preservative and adds flavor and texture to the jam. Do not reduce the amount of sugar called for in jam recipes unless you are prepared to store your jam in the refrigerator. Unless otherwise specified, sugar means white granulated sugar.

For those with special concerns about sugar, it is possible to make sweet preserves using reduced amounts of sugar or sugar substitutes, using modified pectin or gelatin. Special recipes are required.

Pectin: Pectin is a naturally occurring substance found in all fruits. Pectin causes jam to thicken. If all fruits contained the same amounts of pectin, making jam would be a cinch. But the amount of pectin varies not only from one fruit to another, but even within groups of fruits, that is, by variety. The pectin content is also determined by the degree of ripeness of the fruit; even growing conditions can have an effect. A wet year will produce plump, juicy fruit with less pectin; a dry year results in drier, smaller fruit with a higher pectin content. Fruits rich in pectin make good jam quickly and easily. High- and low-pectin fruits can be combined to achieve a desirable pectin level.

Another solution is to use a commercial pectin product. Commercial pectins are made from citrus fruits or apples. They can be used with any fruit to assure the formation of a gel.

This book does not contain many recipes using commercial pectin, as excellent, reliable recipes are found inside every package. I have only included commercial pectin in those recipes where a gel could not be obtained in a reasonable amount of time without it (see next chapter, on Jellies).

Light Pectins

One type of modified pectin that is widely available on the market makes excellent preserves using one-third less sugar. Simply follow the recipes included with the product. Most "light" pectin products also include recipes for no-sugar spreads using sugar substitutes. These recipes produce preserves with a softer set than those made with sugar and have no preservative qualities. They have a short shelf life and must be stored in the refrigerator.

The jams in this chapter are made by the traditional "long cook" method — without the use of commercial pectin. Long-cooked jams use less sugar than those made with commercial pectin and, I believe, have a more intense fruit flavor.

Acid: Jams will not thicken properly without the presence of acid. Many fruits naturally contain sufficient acid, but others require the addition of an acid, usually lemon juice, to help the jam to gel. Underripe fruit has a higher acid content than fully ripe fruit.

Making Jam or Jelly from Frozen Fruit

So many berries ripen at the same time of year! Sometimes it's hard to keep up with jam or jelly making during the summertime, when there is so much to do. If you haven't the time (or the inclination) to make berry jam or jelly in season, you can freeze fresh berries for use at any time of the year.

Berries should be frozen as soon as possible after picking. Rinse the berries and stem or hull them if necessary. Gently pat the berries dry using paper towels. Place the berries in a single layer on trays or cookie sheets lined with waxed paper. Freeze until solid, about 2 hours.

As you are aware, accurate measurements are very important in jam and jelly making. Because frozen berries tend to collapse somewhat as they thaw, it is advisable to measure your berries as you pack them into their containers once they are frozen. Measure the berries in the quantities required for a single recipe. Transfer them to freezer bags or plastic containers, label clearly with the type of berry and the amount, and freeze.

Do not add sugar to fruit that is being frozen for jam and jelly making — berries freeze perfectly well without it.

For the best flavor use frozen berries within one year.

To make jam or jelly using frozen berries, simply remove the measured berries from the freezer and thaw the fruit at room temperature until only a few ice crystals remain. Then just follow your favorite recipe.

The Basics of Making Jam

- Select a mixture of ripe and slightly underripe fruit (¾ ripe to ¼ slightly underripe fruit is a good ratio).

- Rinse or wash the fruit briefly under running water. Do not allow the fruit to soak in water for long periods of time.

- Prepare the fruit as directed in the recipe (peel and/or chop or crush). Some recipes call for precooking hard fruits (such as pears) or stone fruits (such as peaches) briefly, in water or their own juices. Others require you to leave the fruit and sugar to stand for a short time to allow juices to form.

- Bring the jam to a boil. Count the cooking time from the moment the jam starts to boil vigorously.

- Once the jam starts to boil, it should be stirred often to prevent pieces of fruit from sticking to the bottom of the pot.

- Cooking times for jam may vary in minutes depending on the type of fruit and the amount of pectin present. Most jams are ready when the jam holds its shape somewhat on a spoon. It will thicken more as it cools.

- A candy thermometer is useful to indicate when the jam is cooked. The stage is between 218° and 222°F (103° and 105°C) — it varies slightly depending on the pectin content of the fruit. A good median figure is 220°F (104°C). Adjustments may also need to be made for altitude (see page 18). You do not have to be as precise with jam as you do with jelly. You can also use the plate test, described on page 51, if you like.

- When the jam is cooked, remove it from the heat. Stir and skim off any foam that has collected on the surface of the jam (a metal spoon with a shallow bowl does the best job of this). To reduce the amount of foam somewhat, add ½ tsp. (2.5 mL) of butter to the fruit and sugar mixture *before* it starts to boil.

▶ Some recipes call for stirring the jam briefly (2 – 5 minutes) to help prevent pieces of fruit from rising to the surface and floating at the top of the jam. This is usually the case with jams that are made from hard or stone fruits.

▶ Carefully pour or ladle the hot jam into the hot, sterilized jars. You can use a small pitcher or measuring cup for pouring; a ladle and canning jar funnel are more useful for thicker jams. Sterilize all utensils beforehand by placing them in the boiling water along with your preserving jars.

▶ Leave a ½-inch (1.2-cm) head space at the top of the jars. Carefully wipe the rims of the jars to ensure that there is no spilled jam that might interfere with a good seal. Use a clean cloth or paper towel dipped in hot water (you can use the water from the pot that held your jars).

▶ Seal the jars according to the manufacturer's directions.

▶ Process the jars in a boiling water bath for 10 minutes.

Hint: Safeguard Yourself from Burns

Sweet preserves tend to bubble up and spatter during cooking. Use a long-handled spoon and wear oven mitts, rubber gloves or clean cotton gardening gloves to protect your hands.

Accidents can happen. The risk of burns from splashes can be minimized by wearing long-sleeved clothing—and no shorts or sandals either!

Soft Strawberry Jam

Makes about 6 8-oz. (250-mL) jars

This jam is slightly soft and runny, but oh so delicious. The natural, fruity taste of the strawberries really shines through.

Rinse the berries briefly before hulling to keep them from absorbing too much water.

8 cups	sliced strawberries	2 L
6 cups	sugar	1.5 L
⅓ cup	lemon juice	80 mL

Prepare the preserving jars.

In your preserving pot, crush the strawberries lightly with a potato masher. Simmer over medium-low heat for 10 minutes. Add the sugar and lemon juice, stirring until the sugar is dissolved. Increase the heat to medium-high and boil rapidly, stirring often, for 15–20 minutes or until it is slightly thickened. Test for set, if desired.

Remove from the heat. Stir for 2–3 minutes and skim off the foam if necessary. Pour the jam into hot, sterilized jars, leaving ½ inch (1.2 cm) head space. Wipe the rims clean. Seal according to manufacturer's directions. Process the jars in a boiling water bath for 10 minutes.

Strawberry Lime Jam. Add the finely grated zest of one lime to the strawberries during the initial cooking. Substitute lime juice for lemon juice.

Strawberry Mint Jam. After the jam has been removed from the heat and the foam has been skimmed off, stir in 2 Tbsp. (30 mL) chopped fresh mint.

Strawberry Orange Jam. Slice an orange thinly, discarding the ends and seeds. Chop very finely by hand or in a food processor. Add to the strawberries during the initial cooking.

Ruby Red Raspberry Jam

Makes about 4 8-oz. (250-mL) jars

4 cups	raspberries	950 mL
3 cups	sugar	720 mL
1/4 cup	lemon juice	60 mL

Prepare the preserving jars.

In your preserving pot, gently crush the raspberries with a potato masher. Add the sugar and let stand for 1 hour.

Bring to a boil over medium-high heat; stir in the lemon juice. Boil rapidly, stirring often, for 15 – 20 minutes, or until it starts to thicken. Test for set if desired.

Remove from the heat. Stir and skim off the foam if necessary. Pour the jam into hot, sterilized jars, leaving 1/2 inch (1.2 cm) head space. Wipe the rims clean. Seal according to manufacturer's directions. Process the jars in a boiling water bath for 10 minutes.

Blackberry Jam. Simply replace the raspberries with blackberries for a mouth-watering jam.

The fragile raspberry must be handled carefully. Vulnerable to mold once picked, they should be refrigerated and used as soon as possible.

Jumbleberry Jam

Makes about 4 to 5 8-oz. (250-mL) jars

If you freeze extra berries while they are in season, you can make homemade jam at any time of the year. This also will allow you to combine fruits that are generally not in season at the same time. If you use frozen berries, thaw them first.

2 cups	strawberries	475 mL
2 cups	blackberries	475 mL
1 cup	blueberries	240 mL
1 cup	cranberries	240 mL
3½ cups	sugar	840 mL
¼ cup	lemon juice	60 mL

Prepare the preserving jars.

Combine the berries and sugar in your preserving pot. Mash them thoroughly with a potato masher. Add the lemon juice. Bring to a boil over medium heat and simmer, stirring often, 20–25 minutes, or until thickened. Test for set if desired.

Remove from the heat. Stir and skim off the foam if necessary. Pour the jam into hot, sterilized jars, leaving ½ inch (1.2 cm) head space. Wipe the rims clean. Seal according to manufacturer's directions. Process the jars in a boiling water bath for 10 minutes.

True Blueberry Jam

Makes about 4 to 5 8-oz. (250-mL) jars

Select plump, blue-black berries, avoiding any that are shriveled. Wild blueberries are wonderful if you can get them.

6 cups	blueberries	1.5 L
4 cups	sugar	950 mL
¼ cup	lemon juice	60 mL

Prepare the preserving jars.

In your preserving pot, crush the blueberries thoroughly with a potato masher. Add the sugar and lemon juice. Bring to a boil over medium-high heat and boil rapidly, stirring often, for 15–20 minutes. Test for set if desired.

Remove from the heat. Stir and skim off the foam if necessary. Pour the jam into hot, sterilized jars, leaving ½ inch (1.2 cm) head space. Wipe the rims clean. Seal according to manufacturer's directions. Process the jars in a boiling water bath for 10 minutes.

Black and Blue Jam. Replace half the blueberries with blackberries. After crushing berries and adding sugar, let stand for 1 hour. Follow directions for blueberry jam, adding an extra 2 Tbsp. (30 mL) lemon juice and 2 tsp. (10 mL) finely grated lemon zest.

About Blueberries

Wild lowbush blueberries are common in the east, but on the west coast we are more apt to find the highbush cultivated varieties. Wild berries are generally considered to be more flavorful for eating fresh, but either kind are good for preserving.

Although the blueberry closely resembles another wild fruit, the huckleberry, they are not related. Blueberries contain many tiny edible seeds; huckleberries have only 10, but they are large and stony. Huckleberries are tarter than blueberries and are not cultivated.

Blueberries are botanically related to the English bilberry, also known as the whortleberry. The French *myrtille* is the same fruit.

In North America, blueberries are harvested from May to September, but the peak season is in July and August.

Select firm plump berries that are fresh and dry in appearance. Overripe fruit has a dull lifeless look to it. Blueberries range in color from light blue to blue-black, depending on variety. The silver bloom seen on blueberries is a pearly coating that is a natural protective wax.

Blueberries are a pleasure to prepare. There is no peeling, pitting or hulling; just sort them and pick out the odd stem or two.

Blueberries have a long shelf life compared to other berries; they will keep in the refrigerator up to 2 weeks. Wash them just before using.

Spiced Blackberry and Apple Jam

Makes about 5 to 6 8-oz. (250-mL) jars

2 cups	peeled, cored and chopped apples	475 mL
1/2 cup	red wine vinegar	120 mL
1	lemon, zest only, coarsely grated	1
3 cups	blackberries	720 mL
3 cups	sugar	720 mL
1/4 tsp.	each nutmeg, cinnamon and cloves	1.2 mL

Prepare the preserving jars.

Combine the apples, vinegar and lemon zest in your preserving pot. Bring to a boil over medium heat. Cover and simmer for 10 minutes, until the apples begin to soften, stirring occasionally. Stir in the remaining ingredients. Simmer for 20–25 minutes, stirring often, until the jam thickens. Test for set if desired.

Remove from the heat. Stir and skim off the foam if necessary. Pour the jam into hot, sterilized jars, leaving 1/2 inch (1.2 cm) head space. Wipe the rims clean. Seal according to manufacturer's directions. Process the jars in a boiling water bath for 10 minutes.

Hint: Add Apples to Jam

Adding apples to a jam recipe is an excellent way to stretch fresh fruit and you will boost the pectin level at the same time. The unobtrusive flavor of apples will not mask the taste of the other fruit. Be sure to use a variety of apple that breaks down easily when cooked, such as McIntosh, unless you prefer a chunky jam.

Apricot Jam

Makes about 5 to 6 8-oz. (250-mL) jars

4½ cups	pitted, chopped apricots	1.1 L
⅓ cup	apple juice	80 mL
4 cups	sugar	950 mL
2 Tbsp.	lemon juice	30 mL

Because apricots have little natural pectin, apple juice is added to increase the likelihood of a good set. Nevertheless, this will still be a rather soft jam.

Prepare the preserving jars.

Combine the apricots and apple juice in your preserving pot. Bring to a boil over medium heat, cover and simmer about 10 minutes, until the apricots are tender, stirring occasionally.

Add the sugar and lemon juice, stirring until the sugar dissolves. Bring to a full boil over medium-high heat, then reduce the heat to medium. Simmer 15–20 minutes, stirring almost constantly, until the jam has thickened. Test for set if desired.

Remove from the heat and stir for 3–5 minutes. Pour the jam into hot, sterilized jars, leaving ½ inch (1.2 cm) head space. Wipe the rims clean. Seal according to manufacturer's directions. Process the jars in a boiling water bath for 10 minutes.

Apricot Pits and Kernels

If you crack open an apricot pit, you will find a kernel inside that has a strong smell and taste of almonds. Plums, cherries and peaches have such kernels as well.

Many old-time recipes instruct you to place these kernels in a cheese-cloth bag and cook them with the other ingredients to impart an almond flavor to some preserves. This practice is no longer recommended, as these kernels contain a cyanide compound—hydrocyanic acid—which can be toxic.

Although some may say that there is no danger in using just a few kernels, as the amount of hydrocyanic acid would be minimal, I say, why take the chance?

Gingered Pear Jam

Makes about 6 to 7 8-oz. (250-mL) jars

I can eat this straight from the jar! To save time, use a food processor fitted with a shredding disc to chop the pears.

1	3-inch (7.5-cm) cinnamon stick	1
1 tsp.	whole cloves	5 mL
6 cups	peeled, cored and chopped pears	1.5 L
1/4 cup	lemon juice	60 mL
4 1/2 cups	sugar	1.1 L
1/4 cup	chopped candied ginger	60 mL

Prepare the preserving jars. Put the cinnamon stick and cloves into a cheesecloth bag and tie the top with string.

Combine the pears and lemon juice in your preserving pot. Bring to a boil over medium heat. Cover and simmer for 10 minutes, stirring often.

Add the cheesecloth bag of spices and the sugar and ginger; stir until the sugar is dissolved. Cook over medium heat, stirring often, for 20–25 minutes, or until the mixture thickens. Be careful, as the jam may tend to stick to the bottom of the pot towards the end of the cooking time. Test for set if desired.

Remove from the heat and discard the spice bag. Stir the jam and skim off the foam if necessary. Ladle the jam into hot, sterilized jars, leaving 1/2 inch (1.2 cm) head space. Wipe the rims clean. Seal according to manufacturer's directions. Process the jars in a boiling water bath for 10 minutes.

About Cloves

Cloves are the dried, unopened floral buds of a tropical evergreen tree that is a member of the myrtle family. The highly aromatic, spicy-sweet flavor of cloves is indispensable in many varieties of preserves. Whole cloves resemble small tacks. They have a biting sharp flavor; use them sparingly to avoid overwhelming other tastes. Whole cloves are always removed after cooking. Ground cloves are less pungent than whole cloves.

Butterscotch Peach Jam

Makes about 5 to 6 8-oz. (250-mL) jars

6 cups	peeled, cored and chopped peaches	1.5 L
1/3 cup	lemon juice	80 mL
5 cups	brown sugar	1.2 L

Try to select freestone rather than clingstone peaches — they are so much quicker to prepare, as the flesh of the peach easily separates from the pit.

Prepare the preserving jars.

Combine the peaches and lemon juice in your preserving pot. Crush the fruit with a potato masher. Bring to a boil over medium heat, cover and simmer for 10 minutes, stirring occasionally. Stir in the brown sugar. Increase the heat to medium-high and cook, stirring often, for about 20–25 minutes, until slightly thickened. Test for set if desired.

Remove from the heat and stir the jam for 3–5 minutes. Skim off the foam if necessary. Ladle the jam into hot, sterilized jars, leaving 1/2 inch (1.2 cm) head space. Wipe the rims clean. Seal according to manufacturer's directions. Process the jars in a boiling water bath for 10 minutes.

How to Make a Cheesecloth Spice Bag

A cheesecloth bag allows for the easy removal of whole spices from your preserving pot once the preserves are cooked. It is also very useful for straining liquids.

Cheesecloth is a loosely woven, lightweight cloth. You can usually find it at the grocery store.

Cut a double thickness of cheesecloth about 4 inches (10 cm) square. Place the spices in the center and gather up the corners to form a pouch. Tie it tightly at the top with string.

To extract all of the spicy goodness, place the spice bag in a small bowl when you remove it from the preserves. Tilt the bowl over the preserving pot and use the back of a spoon to press the bag and allow all the flavored juices to drip back into the pot. Discard the spice bag.

Peach Melba Jam

Makes about 4 to 5 8-oz. (250-mL) jars

Peach Melba is a classic dessert created by the great French chef, Escoffier, in honor of a famous opera singer named Nellie Melba. Despite the fact that the quantity of peaches is four times that of the raspberries, the raspberry red color will prevail.

4 cups	peeled, pitted and chopped peaches	950 mL
1/4 cup	lemon juice	60 mL
1 cup	raspberries	240 mL
4 cups	sugar	950 mL

Prepare the preserving jars.

Combine the peaches and lemon juice in your preserving pot. Mash thoroughly with a potato masher. Bring to a boil over medium heat. Cover and simmer for 10 minutes, stirring occasionally. Stir in the raspberries and sugar. Increase the heat to medium-high and boil rapidly, stirring often, for 20–25 minutes, or until the jam begins to thicken. Test for set if desired.

Remove from the heat. Stir and skim off the foam if necessary. Pour the jam into hot, sterilized jars, leaving ½ inch (1.2 cm) head space. Wipe the rims clean. Seal according to manufacturer's directions. Process the jars in a boiling water bath for 10 minutes.

About Rhubarb

There are red and green varieties of rhubarb, but both become brown when cooked. Select firm, crisp, thick stalks showing good color. Avoid rhubarb that is limp, stringy or hollow-looking. Rhubarb wilts quickly at room temperature. It will keep refrigerated, in a plastic bag, for 3 to 5 days.

To prepare rhubarb, cut off the root end and pull away any stringy bits. Always be sure to remove all the green leaves from rhubarb stalks—they are toxic. Wash the stalks well and cut them into pieces—most recipes call for 1-inch (2.5-cm) or ½-inch (1.2-cm) dice.

Rhubarb freezes easily. Simply place the washed, chopped rhubarb into freezer bags or plastic containers and freeze. Measure rhubarb before freezing and note the amount on the label to simplify using it in recipes later on.

Strawberry Rhubarb Jam

Makes about 4 to 5 8-oz. (250-mL) jars

3 cups	rhubarb, chopped into ½-inch (1.2-cm) dice	720 mL
4 cups	sugar	950 mL
3 cups	sliced strawberries	720 mL
¼ cup	lemon juice	60 mL

Combine the rhubarb and sugar in your preserving pot. Let stand for 2 hours. Prepare the preserving jars.

Add the strawberries and lemon juice and bring to a boil over medium heat, stirring until the sugar is dissolved. Increase the heat to medium-high and boil rapidly, stirring often, for 20–25 minutes, or until the jam is slightly thickened. Test for set if desired.

Remove from the heat and stir for 3–5 minutes. Skim off the foam if necessary. Pour into hot, sterilized jars, leaving ½ inch (1.2 cm) head space. Wipe the rims clean. Seal according to manufacturer's directions. Process the jars in a boiling water bath for 10 minutes.

One of spring's first crops, rhubarb turns a rather unappetizing brown color when cooked. But team it with strawberries and you have this sweet-tart, rose-colored jam. Use less rhubarb and more strawberries or vice versa, if you prefer.

Rhubarb and Carrot Jam

Makes about 4 8-oz. (250-mL) jars

An unusual combination that tastes terrific, this jam can easily be made at any time of year using frozen rhubarb.

4 cups	rhubarb, chopped into ½-inch (1.2-cm) dice	950 mL
4 cups	grated carrots	950 mL
2	oranges, juice and finely grated zest	2
2	lemons, juice and finely grated zest	2
6 cups	sugar	1.5 L

Mix all the ingredients together in your preserving pot. Cover and let stand overnight.

The next day, bring the mixture to a boil over medium heat, stirring occasionally.

Prepare the preserving jars.

Simmer the mixture for 25–40 minutes, stirring often, until the jam begins to thicken. It is a good idea to use a thermometer to test for set with this jam as the cooking time can vary widely. When the thermometer registers 220°F (104°C), remove from the heat and test again using the plate test (see "How to Test for Gel," page 50). If the jam is not thick enough, cook it a little longer, but stir it constantly, as it may begin to stick to the bottom of the pot.

When the jam is ready, remove it from the heat and stir for 2–3 minutes. Ladle the jam into hot, sterilized jars, leaving ½ inch (1.2 cm) head space. Wipe the rims clean. Seal according to manufacturer's directions. Process the jars in a boiling water bath for 10 minutes.

Facing page, left to right: *Apricot Jam (p.37), Kiwi Lime Jam (p. 44), and Ruby Red Raspberry Jam (p. 33).*

Plum Jam

Makes about 4 to 5 8-oz. (250-mL) jars

2 lbs.	plums, stems removed	900 g
1 cup	water	240 mL
3 cups	sugar	720 mL
2 Tbsp.	lemon juice	30 mL

Prepare the preserving jars.

Combine the plums and water in your preserving pot and bring to a boil over medium heat. Reduce the heat to medium-low. Cover and simmer for about 20 minutes, stirring occasionally, until the plums are soft. The plum pits will rise to the surface; fish them out with a slotted spoon. Add the sugar and lemon juice. Increase the heat to medium and cook, stirring often, for 20–25 minutes, or until thickened. Test for set if desired.

Remove from the heat. Stir and skim off the foam if necessary. Pour into hot, sterilized jars, leaving ½ inch (1.2 cm) head space. Wipe the rims clean. Seal according to manufacturer's directions. Process the jars in a boiling water bath for 10 minutes.

Plum Apple Jam. Replace water with 1 cup (240 mL) apple juice and add 1 lb. (454 g) apples, peeled, cored and coarsely chopped, to your preserving pot. Increase sugar to 4 cups (950 mL) and replace lemon juice with the juice and finely grated zest of 1 whole lemon.

Plums are available in a bewildering variety of colors and sizes. Each has its own distinct flavor. Any type of plum can be used to make this tasty jam, and the nicest thing is, you don't have to peel or chop the fruit.

Facing page, left to right: *Honey Lemon Jelly (p.57), Jalepeño Pepper Jelly (p. 63), and Basic Apple Jelly (p. 53).*

You may do as you choose, but I like to add a couple of drops of green food coloring to this jam. The resulting color, a gorgeous emerald green, is far more attractive than the army green that you'll get without it.

Kiwi Lime Jam

Makes about 3 8-oz. (250-mL) jars

8	large, firm-ripe kiwis	8
2 Tbsp.	finely grated lime zest	30 mL
6 Tbsp.	fresh lime juice	90 mL
3 cups	sugar	720 mL
	a few drops of green food coloring (optional)	

Peel the kiwis and shred them in a food processor, or slice them and then chop finely. Combine all the ingredients except the food coloring in your preserving pot. Let stand for 30 minutes, until the sugar is dissolved and the juices begin to flow.

Prepare the preserving jars.

Bring the fruit to a boil over medium-high heat. Boil rapidly, stirring constantly, for 15–20 minutes. Test for set using a thermometer or the plate test (see "How to Test for Gel," page 50).

Remove from the heat, stir and skim off the foam if necessary. Carefully add 1 or 2 drops of food coloring if desired. (Be judicious in your use of food coloring. Your jam should be a nice, natural *kiwi* green. Start by adding one drop, then stir well and look at the color. Remember, you can always add more, but you can't take it out!)

Pour the jam into hot, sterilized jars, leaving ½ inch (1.2 cm) head space. Wipe the rims clean. Seal according to manufacturer's directions. Process the jars in a boiling water bath for 10 minutes.

Note: One lime will yield approximately 2 Tbsp. (30 mL) of lime juice and 2 tsp. (10 mL) of lime zest.

Jellies

There's no escaping it — making jelly is a little trickier than making jam. The aim of jelly making is to get the stuff to gel — and that requires a little extra care and precision. A runny jam is still jam, but there's no disguising an unset jelly — it's a syrup!

Like jam, jelly requires a careful balance of fruit, pectin, sugar and acid. Fruits that are high in pectin will form a gel naturally; others need the assistance of additional pectin, either homemade or commercially prepared.

It is possible to make your own homemade pectin extract from apples or citrus fruit, but it is a rather time-consuming process. With a few exceptions, the recipes here call for fruits that are rich enough in pectin to form a gel naturally. I have also included a few special recipes that use commercial pectin, as some delicious, popular varieties of jelly simply cannot be made without it.

The traditional method of making jelly involves a two-step process. First, the fruit is simmered in water or its own juice, then the juice is carefully strained away from the fruit pulp. For the richest flavor in the finished jelly, a minimal amount of water is added; this varies according to the juiciness of the fruit.

In the second step, the fruit juice and an appropriate amount of sugar are boiled until the mixture reaches the gel stage. The volume of sugar and the cooking time are dependent on the amount of pectin in the fruit juice.

This method is only suitable for pectin-rich fruits such as apples, quinces and currants. To make jellies from low-pectin fruits, such as strawberries, raspberries or cherries, you must either combine the juice with the juice of a high-pectin fruit, or use a commercial pectin product to assist the gelling process.

Commercial pectin manufacturers include detailed, reliable recipes with their products, which enable you to make jelly from virtually any type of fruit, whether the fruit contains sufficient natural pectin or not. These recipes must be followed to the letter to ensure success. Don't attempt to use commercial pectin recipes without adding the pectin product. They won't work.

The recipes in this book that contain commercial pectin follow the methods recommended by the manufacturers. Don't alter the amounts of fruit or sugar specified in the recipes.

There are two basic varieties of commercial pectin: dry (powdered) pectin, sometimes referred to as pectin crystals, and liquid pectin. Liquid pectin comes in foil-wrapped envelopes, two to a package. When using liquid pectin, be sure to read the recipe carefully to be certain that you are using the correct amount. There is also a relatively new type of dry pectin, specially developed for recipes using reduced amounts of sugar.

Each type of pectin requires that you follow a slightly different procedure — they are not interchangeable in recipes. Dry pectin crystals are mixed with the *unheated* fruit or fruit juice *before* cooking. The sugar is added later on. Liquid pectin is added to the *boiling* fruit or juice and sugar *during* the cooking.

When using commercial pectin, cook for the recommended time, but no longer. You do not increase the likelihood of a gel by prolonging the cooking time, in fact, quite the opposite. For

Using a Jelly Bag

If you are going to make serious amounts of jelly, you may want to invest in a jelly bag. It is easy to manage and can save a considerable amount of messing around.

A jelly bag is a cloth pouch made from a closely woven fabric that, by means of a metal frame, can be suspended over a bowl. It is used for straining cooked fruit in order to achieve a clear juice. Jelly bags can be purchased from cookware shops. However convenient, though, a jelly bag is not essential.

while pectin is activated by heat, it is deactivated by extended cooking.

You will find mention of the term "a full rolling boil" in some recipes, especially those using commercial pectin. A full rolling boil is reached when the jelly mixture is boiling so hard that no matter how much you stir it, the boiling will not subside.

Jellies may take some time to set. Some jellies made using commercial pectin will set within hours, others may take as long as a week or two. It is best to leave jellies undisturbed until they have set firmly.

Easy Steps to Making Jelly
Step 1: Extract the Juice

▸ Use ¾ ripe fruit and ¼ slightly underripe fruit. Jelly can also be made successfully with frozen fruit (see p. 29 for more information).

▸ Wash the fruit briefly in cold water; do not allow the fruit to soak in water.

▸ Cut stone or hard fruits, such as peaches or pears, into small pieces. Do not peel or core fruits, as the peels and cores contain most of the pectin necessary to cause the juice to gel. Berries and small fruits such as grapes are crushed rather than cut up.

▸ Place the prepared fruit in your preserving pot and add the amount of water indicated in the recipe. The harder the fruit, the more water is generally required. Many soft fruits and berries contain sufficient juice so that no additional water is needed.

▸ Cover the pot, bring to a boil and simmer until the fruit is very soft and the juices are flowing. Berries only need about 10–15 minutes; hard fruits may take as long as 30 minutes to cook sufficiently.

▸ Remove the pot from the heat and transfer the mixture to a dampened jelly bag (or a colander lined with a double thickness of cheesecloth) suspended over a large bowl. The clear juice will drip through the bag and into the bowl below, leaving the solids behind. This can be a rather slow process — it is best to allow the juice to drip overnight, or at least several hours. Do not squeeze the bag.

Note: You can prepare the juice one day and make jelly a day or two later. And if you decide that you don't want to make jelly after all, the extracted fruit juice diluted with a little water or soda is an excellent drink. Extracted juice can also be frozen for future jelly-making ventures.

Step 2: Make the Jelly

▸ Measure the juice into your preserving pot and add the amount of sugar called for in the recipe.

▸ You can extract as much juice as you have fruit—in great batches if you like—but do not make jelly using more than 6 cups (1.5 L) of fruit juice at a time. Four cups (950 mL) is usually a good amount. Large volumes of juice have to be boiled for a longer time, decreasing the likelihood of a good set. Also, since the juice and sugar mixture usually triples in volume as it boils, most pots are not large enough to accommodate larger batches. It really doesn't take much longer to cook several batches of jelly and the results will be superior.

▸ Bring the juice and sugar to a boil over high heat, then reduce the heat slightly if necessary to keep the pot from boiling over. Boil rapidly, stirring often to prevent scorching. You can greatly reduce the amount of foam by adding ½ tsp. (2.5 mL) of butter to the mixture *before* it starts to boil.

- Insert a thermometer in the boiling liquid once it starts to get syrupy. The jelly is done when it reaches 220°F (104°C), or 8°F (4°C) above the boiling point of water at your elevation. You may also determine doneness by using gel tests, described below. (Remove the jelly from the heat while performing a gel test.)

- Remove the pot from the heat and skim any foam off the surface of the jelly.

- Stir the jelly briefly and pour it into hot, sterilized jars. Process the jars in a boiling water bath for 5 minutes. The processing time for jelly is the briefest of any type of preserve as the heat from the boiling water bath can penetrate the liquid jelly very quickly.

- Once processed, allow jellies to stand undisturbed until they are set. Some may take as long as 48 hours. Sometimes jellies made with commercial pectin can take up to 2 weeks to set — believe it or not!

How to Test for Gel

The following tests will help you to determine if your preserves have cooked sufficiently to form a gel. You can use a combination of tests to be extra sure.

When you are performing either the plate or sheet test, remove the pot from the heat so that the mixture doesn't continue to cook. If your gel test fails, cook the mixture a little longer, then try again. Keep cooking and testing until the mixture passes the test.

The temperature test: Using a candy or jelly thermometer is the easiest and most accurate method. Stir the hot mixture, then immerse the thermometer in it, making sure that the bulb does not touch the bottom of the pot. Continue cooking until the temperature reaches 220°F (104°C), or 8°F (4°C) above the temperature of boiling water at your elevation.

The cold plate test: Place a small plate in the freezer. Towards the end of the cooking time, place a spoonful of the hot mixture on the plate. Return the plate to the freezer for 2 minutes, then check to see if the mixture has gelled.

The sheet test: This is the traditional method for jellies, but it's not recommended for jams. The sheet test can be tricky for beginners, because it may not be obvious what you are looking for. Dip a cold metal spoon into the boiling mixture, then raise it above the pot, away from the steam. Wait about 20 seconds, then slowly tilt the spoon and allow the mixture to drip off the spoon and back into the pot. If the mixture forms 2 drops that flow together to form a "sheet" (a wide drop that sort of hangs from the spoon), then the gel stage has been reached.

Jelly Troubles

Sometimes things can go wrong, no matter how careful you are. Here are some possible explanations as to why your jelly may be less than perfect.

Failure to set

▸ Fruit lacked pectin or acid.

▸ Jelly was overcooked, causing pectin to break down.

Jelly That Fails to Set

It sometimes happens that jelly just won't gel — no matter how long you cook it. If your jelly will not sheet from a spoon or pass the plate test, even though it has reached the gel point according to your thermometer, it probably isn't going to gel. More cooking will only make it gluey and gummy, so give up gracefully.

Runny fruit jelly makes a lovely thick syrup for pancakes or desserts. Savory "jelly" can be used as a glaze for roast meats or to enhance sauces.

- ▸ Jelly was undercooked; too little evaporation caused a weak set.
- ▸ Too much water was added during juice extraction.
- ▸ Insufficient sugar was used.

Crystallization

- ▸ Too much sugar was used.
- ▸ There was too little acid.
- ▸ Jelly was overcooked.
- ▸ There was a delay in sealing the jars.
- ▸ Tartrate crystals were present (in grape jelly).

Cloudy jelly

- ▸ The jelly bag was squeezed, forcing particles of fruit pulp into the juice.
- ▸ Too much underripe fruit was used (it contains more starch than sugar).

"Weeping" jelly (liquid separates from the solids)

- ▸ There was too much acid.

Mold

- ▸ Improper sterilization.
- ▸ Jars were poorly sealed.

Always discard moldy jelly!

Basic Apple Jelly

Makes about 4 to 5 8-oz. (250-mL) jars

| 3 lbs. | tart, firm apples | 1.4 kg |
| | sugar | |

Chop the apples coarsely, removing the stems and blossom ends. Do not peel or core. Place the apples in your preserving pot, adding enough water to completely cover the fruit, about 5 cups (1.2 L).

Cover the pot and bring to a boil over medium heat. Simmer for 20–25 minutes, stirring occasionally, until the apples are very soft. Crush the apples using a potato masher and cook for another 2–3 minutes. Remove from the heat.

Transfer the mixture to a dampened jelly bag or a colander lined with a double thickness of cheesecloth. Let the juice drip through overnight.

The next day, measure the juice; there should be about 4 cups (950 mL). Discard the pulp. Prepare the preserving jars.

In your processing pot, combine the apple juice and ¾ cup (180 mL) of sugar for each cup (240 mL) of juice. Bring to a boil over high heat and boil rapidly, stirring constantly, for 15–20 minutes, or until the mixture starts to get syrupy. Test for gel and when the gel stage has been reached, remove from the heat. Stir and skim off the foam if necessary.

Pour the jelly into hot, sterilized jars, leaving ½ inch (1.2 cm) head space. Wipe the rims clean. Seal according to manufacturer's directions. Process the jars in a boiling water bath for 5 minutes.

Spiced Apple Jelly. Add one 2- to 3-inch (5- to 7.5-cm) cinnamon stick (broken), 2 tsp. (10 mL) whole cloves, 1 tsp. (5 mL) whole allspice and ½ cup (120 mL) cider vinegar to the apples during the initial cooking.

A classic jelly, apple jelly can be used as a base for many varieties of herbal jelly as well. To make crabapple jelly, just substitute an equal amount of red-skinned crabapples for the apples.

Apple Mint Jelly

Makes about 4 to 5 8-oz. (250-mL) jars

3 lbs.	firm, tart apples	1.4 kg
1	lemon	1
1	small bunch of fresh mint, roughly chopped, about 1—1½ cups (240—360 mL)	1
1 cup	cider vinegar	240 mL
	sugar	

Chop the apples coarsely, removing the stems and blossom ends. Do not peel or core. Cut the lemon in half lengthwise and slice it thinly. Place the apples and lemon in your preserving pot and add just enough water to barely cover the fruit.

Cover the pot and bring to a boil over medium heat. Simmer for 20–25 minutes, stirring occasionally, until the apples are very soft. Add the chopped mint and vinegar and simmer for another 10 minutes. Remove from the heat.

Crush the mixture with a potato masher, then cover the pot and let stand for 10 minutes. Transfer the mixture to a jelly bag or a colander lined with a double thickness of cheesecloth. Let the juice drip through overnight.

The next day, prepare the preserving jars. Measure the juice; there should be about 5 cups (1.2 L). Combine the juice and an equal amount of sugar in your preserving pot. Bring to a boil over high heat and boil rapidly, stirring constantly, for 15–20 minutes, or until the jelly tests done.

Remove from the heat. Stir and skim off the foam if necessary. Pour the jelly into hot, sterilized jars, leaving ½ inch (1.2 cm) head space. Wipe the rims clean. Seal according to manufacturer's directions. Process the jars in a boiling water bath for 5 minutes.

A natural accompaniment to roast lamb or chops, this versatile jelly also makes a lovely glaze for fresh fruit tarts. I consider its golden color to be most appealing, but if you must have it green, stir in a couple of drops of green food coloring just before it goes into the jars.

Apple Lemon Balm Jelly. Substitute 1 – 1½ cups (240 – 360 mL) chopped fresh lemon balm for the mint.

Apple Basil Jelly. Substitute 1 – 1½ cups (240 – 360 mL) chopped fresh basil for the mint.

Apple Rose Geranium Jelly. Substitute 1 – 1½ (240 – 360 mL) chopped rose geranium leaves for the mint.

Cranberry and Apple Jelly

Makes about 4 to 5 8-oz. (250-mL) jars

3 cups	cranberries	720 mL
6	large apples, coarsely chopped	6
	sugar	

You can use either fresh or frozen cranberries for this delectable jelly. It is tart enough to accompany roast meats.

Combine the cranberries and apples in your preserving pot. Add enough water to cover the fruit. Cover the pot and bring to a boil over medium heat. Simmer for 20 – 25 minutes, stirring occasionally, until the fruit is very soft. Crush the fruit using a potato masher and cook for another 2 – 3 minutes. Remove from the heat. Transfer the mixture to a dampened jelly bag or a sieve lined with a double thickness of cheesecloth. Let the juice drip through overnight.

The next day, measure the juice; there should be about 4 cups (950 mL). Discard the pulp. Prepare the preserving jars.

In your preserving pot, combine the juice with an equal amount of sugar. Bring to a boil over high heat and boil rapidly, stirring constantly, for about 15 minutes, or until the jelly tests done.

Remove from the heat, stir and skim off the foam if necessary. Pour the jelly into hot, sterilized jars, leaving ½ inch (1.2 cm) head space. Wipe the rims clean. Seal according to manufacturer's directions. Process the jars in a boiling water bath for 5 minutes.

Quince Jelly Scented with Vanilla

Makes about 4 to 5 8-oz. (250-mL) jars

4 lbs.	quinces, cut into pieces	1.8 kg
1	vanilla bean	1
	sugar	
2 Tbsp.	lemon juice	30 mL

Rather a forgotten, old-fashioned fruit, quinces are rarely available in markets or fruit stands. I'd never seen a quince until I discovered them growing in my own yard! A splendid ornamental shrub with lovely red flowers, quinces mature in the autumn and when they are ripe have an incredible fragrance.

Quinces are so hard and astringent they are not usually eaten raw. They remain hard even when ripe, which makes them rather difficult to prepare. Rub off any fuzz on the skin of the fruit using a dry towel. Wash and remove the stems and blossom ends, but do not peel or core. Cut them into small pieces.

Place the quince pieces and the vanilla bean in your preserving pot and add enough water to completely cover them. Cover and bring to a boil over medium heat. Simmer, stirring occasionally, for about 45 minutes, until the quinces are very soft. Mash the quince pulp with a potato masher and cook for another 5 minutes. Remove from the heat. Remove the vanilla bean.

Transfer the mixture to a dampened jelly bag or a colander lined with a double thickness of cheesecloth. Let the juice drip through overnight.

The next day, measure the juice; there should be about 4 cups (950 mL). Discard the pulp. Prepare the preserving jars.

In your preserving pot, combine the quince juice and ¾ cup (180 mL) sugar for each 1 cup (240 mL) of juice. Add the lemon juice. Bring to a boil over high heat and boil rapidly, stirring often, for about 20–25 minutes, or until the jelly tests done. Stir more often towards the end of the cooking time to prevent scorching.

Remove from the heat, stir and skim off foam if necessary. Pour the jelly into hot, sterilized jars, leaving ½ inch (1.2 cm) head space. Wipe the rims clean. Seal according to manufacturer's directions. Process the jars in a boiling water bath for 5 minutes.

Note: If you cannot use a vanilla bean, substitute ½ tsp. (2.5 mL) pure vanilla extract, adding it just before the jelly is poured into the jars.

Honey Lemon Jelly

Makes about 3 to 4 8-oz. (250-mL) jars

2 cups	honey	475 mL
1 cup	sugar	240 mL
2/3 cup	freshly squeezed lemon juice, strained	160 mL
2 tsp.	finely grated lemon zest	10 mL
1/2 cup	water	120 mL
1	3-oz. (85-mL) pouch liquid pectin	1

Prepare the preserving jars.

Combine the honey, sugar, lemon juice, lemon zest, and water in your preserving pot. Bring to a boil over medium heat and stir in the pectin. Continue to cook and stir until the mixture reaches a full, rolling boil that cannot be stirred down. Boil hard for exactly 1 minute. Remove from the heat, stir and skim off the foam if necessary.

Quickly pour the jelly into hot, sterilized jars, leaving 1/2 inch (1.2 cm) head space. Wipe the rims clean. Seal according to manufacturer's directions. Process the jars in a boiling water bath for 5 minutes.

Use a light, delicately flavored honey for this magically sweet treat. There are two important things to note about this jelly. Honey jelly really boils up when it is cooking so take care that the pot does not boil over. It also sets up very quickly when it is removed from the heat, so do not delay in filling the jars.

About Vanilla

Vanilla comes from the pod fruit of a vine native to Central America, a member of the orchid family. Vanilla must be hand-pollinated and has a long, complex curing process, which explains why it is so expensive.

Vanilla pods, or beans, have a superior flavor to vanilla extract, but pure vanilla extract is infinitely preferable to a synthetic substitute.

Although expensive, vanilla beans are well worth the price. They will keep for months in an airtight container; stored in a canister of sugar, a vanilla bean will impart a rich mellow flavor to the sugar. Vanilla beans may be used many times over, as long as they are carefully washed and dried after each use.

Grape Jelly

Makes about 4 to 5 8-oz. (250-mL) jars

Grapes naturally contain tartaric acid which will form crystals in the finished jelly if you do not allow the juice to settle after it is extracted. Do not omit this extra step.

4 lbs.	dark red or blue grapes	1.8 kg
1	tart apple	1
¾ cup	water	180 mL
	sugar	

Stem the grapes and coarsely chop the apple, removing the stem and blossom ends. Combine the grapes, apple and water in your preserving pot. Cover and bring to a boil over medium heat. Simmer for about 20 minutes, stirring occasionally, until the fruit is very soft. Remove from the heat.

Transfer the mixture to a dampened jelly bag or a colander lined with a double thickness of cheesecloth. Let the juice drip through overnight. Cover the juice and refrigerate for 8–10 hours to allow the tartrate crystals to settle to the bottom of the pot. Strain the juice a second time, taking great care not to disturb the sediment. Discard the sediment.

Prepare the preserving jars.

Measure the juice into your preserving pot; there should be about 4 cups (950 mL). Add ¾ cup (180 mL) of sugar for each 1 cup (240 mL) of juice. Bring to a boil over high heat and boil rapidly, stirring constantly, for about 15–20 minutes, or until the jelly tests done.

Remove from the heat, stir and skim off the foam if necessary. Pour the jelly into hot, sterilized jars, leaving ½ inch (1.2 cm) head space. Wipe the rims clean. Seal according to manufacturer's directions. Process the jars in a boiling water bath for 5 minutes.

Facing page: *Peach, Mango, Nectarine or Papaya Butter (p.114).*

Blackberry Jelly

Makes about 4 8-oz. (250-mL) jars

10 cups	blackberries	2.4 L
½ cup	water	120 mL
3 Tbsp.	lemon juice	45 mL
	sugar	

Also known as bramble jelly, blackberry jelly is an excellent choice for those who love the taste of fresh blackberries, but cannot tolerate the seediness of blackberry jam.

In your preserving pot, crush the blackberries with a potato masher. Add the water and lemon juice. Cover and simmer over medium heat for 15 minutes, stirring occasionally, until the blackberries are really mushy. Remove from the heat.

Transfer the mixture to a dampened jelly bag or a colander lined with a double thickness of cheesecloth. Let the juice drip through overnight.

The next day, measure the juice; there should be about 4 cups (950 mL). Discard the pulp. Prepare the preserving jars.

In your preserving pot, combine the juice and an equal amount of sugar. Bring to a boil over high heat and boil rapidly, stirring often, for about 15–20 minutes, or until the jelly tests done.

Remove from the heat, stir and skim off the foam if necessary. Pour the jelly into hot, sterilized jars, leaving ½ inch (1.2 cm) head space. Wipe the rims clean. Seal according to manufacturer's directions. Process the jars in a boiling water bath for 5 minutes.

Facing page: *Pineapple, Strawberry and Rhubarb Dessert Sauce (p.99).*

Summer Berry Jelly

Makes about 4 to 5 8-oz. (250-mL) jars

A happy marriage of four of summer's finest fruits. The gooseberries provide the pectin necessary to achieve a good set.

2 cups	cherries, stemmed and pitted	475 mL
2 cups	raspberries	475 mL
2 cups	strawberries, hulled	475 mL
2 cups	gooseberries	475 mL
	sugar	
2 Tbsp.	lemon juice	30 mL

Place the fruit in your preserving pot and crush it with a potato masher. Add just enough water to barely cover the fruit. Bring to a boil over medium heat. Cover and simmer for about 15 minutes, stirring occasionally, until the fruit is very soft. Remove from the heat.

Transfer the mixture to a dampened jelly bag or a colander lined with a double thickness of cheesecloth. Let the juice drip through overnight.

The next day, measure the juice; there should be about 4 cups (950 mL). Discard the pulp. Prepare the preserving jars.

In your preserving pot, combine the juice and an equal amount of sugar. Add the lemon juice. Bring to a boil over high heat and boil rapidly, stirring constantly, for about 10 – 15 minutes, or until the jelly tests done.

Remove from the heat, stir and skim off the foam if necessary. Pour the jelly into hot, sterilized jars, leaving ½ inch (1.2 cm) head space. Wipe the rims clean. Seal according to manufacturer's directions. Process the jars in a boiling water bath for 5 minutes.

Red Currant Jelly

Makes about 5 to 6 8-oz. (250-mL) jars

4 lbs.	red currants	1.8 kg
1 cup	water	240 mL
	sugar	

A brilliant red jewel-like jelly with a tart flavor, Red Currant Jelly is traditionally served with meats. There is no need to stem the currants when preparing the juice.

Place the currants in your preserving pot, and crush them, using a potato masher. Add the water and simmer over medium heat until the currants are soft, about 10 minutes. Remove from the heat.

Transfer the pulp to a dampened jelly bag or a colander lined with a double thickness of cheesecloth, and allow to drip through overnight.

The next day, prepare the preserving jars.

Measure the juice into your preserving pot, adding ¾ cup (180 mL) of sugar for each 1 cup (240 mL) of juice. Bring to a boil over high heat and boil rapidly, stirring constantly, for about 10–15 minutes, or until the jelly tests done.

Remove from the heat. Stir and skim off the foam if necessary. Pour the jelly into hot, sterilized jars, leaving ½ inch (1.2 cm) head space. Wipe the rims clean. Seal according to manufacturer's directions. Process the jars in a boiling water bath for 5 minutes.

Adding Chopped Herbs to Jelly

You can add fresh chopped herbs to your jelly after the jelly has been removed from the heat.

Once you have skimmed off the foam, add ¾–1 cup (180–240 mL) fresh chopped herbs, such as basil, mint or tarragon. Stirring for 3–5 minutes will help keep the herbs suspended in the jelly, but they do tend to float to the top. You can tilt the jars from time to time as the jelly cools to distribute the herbs more evenly.

What is commonly known as pepper jelly, or even pepper jam, is actually more of a jellied relish. For those who may be unfamiliar with the substance by any name, it is a truly addictive snack when served with cream cheese and crackers. This version contains orange juice and zest for a little extra zip. You must use a food processor for this recipe because the peppers must be ground finely enough to extract some juice, and this cannot be achieved by simple chopping.

Red Pepper and Orange Jelly

Makes about 6 to 7 8-oz. (250-mL) jars

3 – 4	medium-large red bell peppers	3 – 4
1¼ cups	cider vinegar	300 mL
¼ cup	orange juice	60 mL
¼ cup	finely grated orange zest	60 mL
6 cups	sugar	1.5 L
2	3-oz. (85-mL) pouches liquid pectin	2
½ – 1 tsp.	hot pepper sauce, to taste	2.5 – 5 mL

It's tricky to say how many peppers this will take because they vary so much in size. Cut them into small chunks, discarding the stems, ribs and seeds. Purée in a food processor until finely and uniformly chopped. Use a spatula to scrape down the sides of the bowl once or twice during processing. Measure out 2 cups (475 mL).

Prepare the preserving jars.

Combine the peppers, vinegar, orange juice, zest and sugar in your preserving pot. Bring to a boil over high heat. Reduce the heat to low, cover and simmer for 10 minutes. Increase the heat to high and bring the mixture to a full boil, stirring constantly. Stir in the pectin. Continue to stir over high heat until the mixture returns to a full boil, then boil hard for 1 minute.

Remove from the heat and stir in the hot pepper sauce. Skim off the foam if necessary. Stir for 3–5 minutes (this helps to keep the peppers and zest from floating to the tops of the jars).

Pour the jelly into hot, sterilized jars, leaving ½ inch (1.2 cm) head space. Wipe the rims clean. Seal according to manufacturer's directions. Process the jars in a boiling water bath for 5 minutes.

Jalapeño Pepper Jelly

Makes about 6 to 7 8-oz. (250-mL) jars

25 – 30	medium jalapeño peppers	25 – 30
1½ cups	cider vinegar	360 mL
6½ cups	sugar	1.6 L
½ tsp.	salt	2.5 mL
2	3-oz. (85-mL) pouches liquid pectin	2
	a few drops of green food coloring (optional)	

To prepare the peppers, cut them into chunks, discarding the ribs, stems and seeds. (See "Handling Hot Peppers," page 118.) Chop the pepper chunks in the food processor until they are finely and uniformly ground. Measure out 2 cups (475 mL).

Prepare the preserving jars.

Combine the 2 cups (475 mL) of peppers, vinegar, sugar and salt in your preserving pot. Bring to a boil over high heat, stirring occasionally. Once the mixture has reached a full boil, stir constantly. Boil for 5 minutes. Stir in the pectin, and when the mixture has returned to a full rolling boil, boil for exactly 1 minute.

Remove from the heat. Stir and skim off any foam from the surface of the jelly. Stir the jelly for 3 – 5 minutes (this will help keep the peppers from floating to the tops of the jars). At this time, add the food coloring, if desired. (If you don't mind the drab olive green color of cooked green peppers, or have objections to the use of food coloring, by all means leave it out. But I must confess, I find the jelly to be much prettier if it is included.)

Pour the jelly into hot, sterilized jars, leaving ½ inch (1.2 cm) head space. Wipe the rims clean. Seal according to manufacturer's directions. Process the jars in a boiling water bath for 5 minutes.

No joke — this stuff is really hot! To make a milder version, simply reduce the amount of jalapeño pepper and substitute an equal volume of green pepper. As long as the total volume of peppers is equal to 2 cups (475 mL), it doesn't matter what kind they are.

Rosemary and Red Wine Jelly with Orange

Makes about 4 to 5 8-oz. (250-mL) jars

3/4 cup	fresh rosemary leaves, chopped	180 mL
1	orange, zest only, removed in thin strips	1
2 cups	red wine	475 mL
1/2 cup	red wine vinegar	120 mL
4 cups	sugar	950 mL
1	3-oz. (85-mL) pouch liquid pectin	1

This is a distinguished jelly with an assertive rosemary flavor. Use a robust, full-bodied red wine — the intensity of flavor and color of the jelly depend on using a wine with character.

Rinse the rosemary under running water, shake well, then pat dry with paper towels. Strip the rosemary leaves from the stems, measure and chop coarsely.

Place the rosemary leaves in your preserving pot. Twist the strips of orange zest (as if you were twisting lemon zest to drop into a martini) over the pot to extract the fragrant drops of oil in the skin. Drop the zest into the pot. Add the wine and vinegar and bring to a boil over high heat. As soon as it boils, remove from the heat. Cover the pot and let the mixture steep for 30 minutes.

Strain the mixture through a sieve lined with a double thickness of dampened cheesecloth, pressing on the herbs to extract as much liquid as possible. Discard the herbs. Prepare the preserving jars.

Combine the extracted liquid and the sugar in your preserving pot. Bring to a boil over high heat, stirring often. When the mixture reaches a full boil, stir in the pectin. Cook and stir until the mixture reaches a full rolling boil that cannot be stirred down. Boil hard for exactly 1 minute, stirring constantly. Remove from the heat. Stir and skim off any foam that has formed.

Pour the jelly into the hot, sterilized jars, leaving ½ inch (1.2 cm) head space. Wipe the rims clean. Seal according to manufacturer's directions. Process the jars in a boiling water bath for 5 minutes.

Rosemary and Red Wine Jelly with Garlic. Omit the orange and add 3 – 4 sliced garlic cloves with the rosemary.

Rosemary and Orange Jelly. Substitute orange juice for the wine and 3 Tbsp. (45 mL) lemon juice for the vinegar. Add 1 Tbsp. (15 mL) finely grated orange zest when the jelly is removed from the heat. Stir 3 – 5 minutes to distribute the zest evenly in the jelly.

Glaze a Fresh Fruit Tart with Jelly

For a 9- or 10-inch (23- to 25-cm) fresh fruit tart, melt ½ cup (120 mL) of jelly with about 1 Tbsp. (15 mL) water or juice over low heat, stirring until smooth.

Brush the warm mixture over the cooled tart. Sprinkle with chopped nuts, if desired. When the glaze has set, the tart is ready to serve.

Marmalades

The word *marmalade* is said to derive from the Portuguese word for quince, *marmelo*. A marmalade is a soft jam or jelly-like preserve based on citrus fruit, usually oranges. Marmalades may be thick and chunky or soft and tender. The texture depends on the method used to soften the citrus skin before the marmalade is cooked.

The bitter Seville orange is the principal ingredient in traditional English marmalade, but marmalades may be made from any citrus fruit: oranges, lemons, limes, grapefruits or tangerines, either singly or in combination. Delightful marmalade may also be prepared by partnering citrus fruits with compatible fruits or vegetables... everything from apples to zucchini. Some marmalades are flavored with ginger or other spices, or enhanced by the addition of liqueurs or a good Scotch whiskey!

To my mind, one of the nicest things about marmalade is its season, January to February. Citrus fruit is at its finest at this time of year and also at its most inexpensive. And this is the only time you can find the elusive Seville orange, prized by marmalade enthusiasts for its thin skin, acidic flavor and high pectin content.

After the excitement of Christmas is over, there is no better way to brighten up a dull January day than to bring home a basket of citrus fruit from the market and set to work making marmalade. By happy coincidence, the beginning of the year is always a quiet time on the preserving calendar, so you won't be distracted by other fruits and vegetables clamoring for your attention.

Marmalade does require a little extra time to make, as there are some preliminary preparations that must be done to ensure that your marmalading venture is a successful one.

Some marmalades may take a couple of days to prepare. This is because the tough skin of the citrus fruit needs to be softened before it can be made into marmalade. This may be achieved by soaking the fruit for several hours or overnight and by precooking the fruit in water prior to adding the sugar. Some recipes call for boiling the fruit whole, then chopping it up; in other recipes, the fruit is very thinly sliced, then precooked. A third method involves boiling the zest in several changes of water, then cooking the zest, pulp and juice with water.

In some ways, making marmalade is less complicated than making jam or jelly. Citrus fruits contain plenty of pectin, so there is little danger the marmalade will fail to set. In fact, many marmalades will thicken considerably after cooling, so care must be taken not to overcook them.

Once the peel is softened, it is cooked until tender and the sugar is added. The process moves quickly after this. It is best to use a candy thermometer to gauge the progress of your marmalade as it can reach the gel stage quite quickly. Upon reaching the gel stage, the marmalade must immediately be removed from the heat, skimmed free of foam if necessary, and stirred briefly for a few minutes. The stirring helps to distribute the fruit or zest evenly throughout the mixture.

Not all marmalades are bittersweet. The addition of non-citrus fruit can temper the traditional bitterness of marmalade, making it more palatable to the uninitiated. Once you develop a taste for it, however, you will appreciate the complex flavors and distinctive tang that define a true marmalade.

Traditional English Marmalade

Makes about 5 to 6 8-oz. (250-mL) jars

Early in January keep your eyes peeled for bittersweet Seville oranges, the principal ingredient in this recipe. They have a very short season and can be difficult to find. Be sure to make enough to last the whole year through!

2 lbs.	Seville oranges	900 g
3	medium-sized lemons	3
8 cups	sugar	2 L

Prepare the preserving jars.

Scrub the oranges and lemons well and discard the little stem ends. In your preserving pot, place the *whole* oranges and lemons, and add enough water to cover them. Cover the pot and bring to a boil over medium heat. Simmer for 1–1½ hours, or until the fruit can be easily pierced with a metal skewer. Drain the fruit in a colander, reserving the liquid. When the fruit is cool enough to handle, slice it in half lengthwise. Then place the cut side down and slice very thinly, reserving the seeds. Place the seeds in a cheesecloth bag.

Pour the reserved liquid back into the pot and add the sugar. Cook and stir over low heat until the sugar is dissolved. Increase the heat to medium and simmer the liquid for 10 minutes, stirring often. Stir in the sliced fruit and the bag of seeds. Boil and stir until the marmalade reaches the gel point, about 25 – 30 minutes. Test for gel using the thermometer or plate test.

Remove from the heat and discard the bag of seeds, squeezing it out well first. Skim any foam that may have formed and stir for 2 – 3 minutes to distribute the fruit evenly. Pour the marmalade into hot, sterilized jars, leaving ½ inch (1.2 cm) head space. Wipe the rims clean. Seal according to manufacturer's directions. Process the jars in a boiling water bath for 10 minutes.

Spirited Seville Marmalade. Stir in 3 Tbsp. (45 mL) orange-flavored liqueur, such as Cointreau or Triple Sec, or the same amount of Scotch whiskey just before the marmalade is poured into the jars.

Dark Seville Marmalade. Substitute dark brown sugar for the regular sugar and add 1 Tbsp. (15 mL) molasses when the sugar is added.

Orange Marmalade

Makes about 6 to 7 8-oz. (250-mL) jars

A lively fresh flavor is the hallmark of this popular marmalade.

2 cups	orange slices (2 – 3 medium oranges)	475 mL
2 cups	lemon slices (about 3 medium lemons)	475 mL
6 cups	water	1.5 L
	sugar	

Prepare the preserving jars.

To prepare the fruit, cut the oranges and lemons in half lengthwise, then into quarters. Slice them as thinly as possible, discarding the ends. Place the seeds in a cheesecloth bag.

Combine the orange, lemon, the bag of seeds and the water in your preserving pot. Bring to a boil over high heat. Reduce the heat to medium and simmer until the fruit is tender, about 30 – 40 minutes. Remove from the heat. Discard the bag of seeds, squeezing it out well first.

Measure the fruit and liquid and add an equal volume of sugar to the pot. Bring to a boil over medium-high heat and boil, stirring often, for 20 – 30 minutes. Test for the gel stage using a thermometer or the plate test.

Remove from the heat. Skim off the foam if necessary. Stir for 3 – 5 minutes to prevent floating fruit. Pour the marmalade into hot, sterilized jars, leaving ½ inch (1.2 cm) head space. Wipe the rims clean. Seal according to manufacturer's directions. Process the jars in a boiling water bath for 10 minutes.

Lemon-Lime Marmalade

Makes about 6 to 7 8-oz. (250-mL) jars

A true tart and tangy marmalade. Not for the faint of heart! The skin of the lime is extremely tough; be sure to slice the fruit very thinly.

2 cups	lemon slices (about 3 medium lemons)	475 mL
2 cups	lime slices (about 4 medium limes)	475 mL
7 cups	water	1.75 L
	sugar	

Prepare the preserving jars.

To prepare the fruit, cut the lemons and limes in half lengthwise, then again into quarters. Slice the fruit as thinly as possible, discarding the ends. Place the seeds in a cheese-cloth bag.

Combine the fruit, the bag of seeds and the water in your preserving pot. Cover and let stand at room temperature overnight.

The next day, bring to a boil over high heat, then reduce the heat to medium and simmer until the fruit is very tender, about 45–50 minutes. Remove from the heat. Discard the bag of seeds, squeezing it out as much as possible.

Measure the fruit and liquid. Add an equal volume of sugar. Bring to a boil over medium-high heat and boil, stirring often, for 25–35 minutes. Test for the gel stage using a thermometer or the plate test.

Remove from the heat. Skim off the foam if necessary. Stir for 3–5 minutes to prevent floating fruit. Pour the marmalade into hot, sterilized jars, leaving ½ inch (1.2 cm) head space. Wipe the rims clean. Seal according to manufacturer's directions. Process the jars in a boiling water bath for 10 minutes.

About Lemons

Lemons are an invaluable asset to the home preserver. Although in North America we generally don't preserve lemons on their own, they are probably used in more preserving recipes than any other fruit.

In many recipes, lemons provide the necessary acidity that, in conjunction with pectin and sugar, causes sweet preserves to form a gel. Lemon juice is often added to raise the acidity of low-acid foods to a level that allows those foods to be safely processed in a boiling water bath.

Lemons are also used as a flavor enhancer. A touch of lemon juice will heighten the taste of most foods, sweet or savory. Grated lemon zest enlivens many preserves, conserves and chutneys.

Lemon juice, when sprinkled over cut fruits such as apples, bananas and pears, helps to inhibit browning. Such foods may also be placed in an acidic "bath" of water and lemon juice for the same effect. Lemon juice can also be useful as a mild bleaching agent that helps to keep white vegetables from discoloring during cooking.

Choose plump, firm lemons that feel slightly oily to the touch. They should be bright yellow with no traces of green.

The best lemons will feel heavy for their size and have a fine-textured skin. Thicker-skinned lemons that are lighter generally contain less juice, but are easier to grate for their zest.

In recipes that call for both juice and zest, always grate the zest first, before halving the fruit and extracting the juice. The zest contains the desirable aromatic oils. Avoid the white pith as much as possible; it is very bitter. A vegetable peeler may be helpful in removing large pieces of zest, and a zester is a useful cook's tool that will remove the zest in long thin shreds.

If you wish to extract the juice of a whole lemon, it helps to soften the fruit first by rolling it around on a table or countertop beneath the palm of your hand. The juice will flow more freely, and you will get more of it. Room-temperature lemons will yield more juice than those straight from the refrigerator.

One medium-sized lemon will yield about 2½ – 3 Tbsp. (38 – 45 mL) juice and about 1 Tbsp. (15 mL) grated zest.

Amber Marmalade

Makes about 7 to 8 8-oz. (250-mL) jars

6	medium oranges	6
1	medium lemon	1
2	medium limes	2
4 cups	water	950 mL
4 cups	pineapple, cut in 1/2-inch (1.2-cm) dice	950 mL
	sugar	
1/2 tsp.	ground ginger	2.5 mL

Cut the oranges, lemon and limes in half lengthwise. Placing the cut side down, slice the fruit very thinly, discarding the ends. Place the seeds in a cheesecloth bag. Combine the sliced fruit, water and the bag of seeds in your preserving pot. Cover and cook over low heat for 1 hour, stirring occasionally. Remove from the heat, uncover and cool. When cool, replace the cover and let stand at room temperature overnight.

The next day, squeeze out the cheesecloth bag and discard. Bring the mixture to a boil over medium heat. Add the pineapple. Simmer, partially covered, for about 35–40 minutes, or until the pineapple is tender. Stir occasionally.

Remove the mixture from the heat. Prepare the preserving jars. Measure the fruit mixture and add an equal volume of sugar to the pot. Stir in the ginger. Return to the heat, stirring constantly until the sugar dissolves. Increase the heat to medium-high and cook rapidly, stirring often, for 15–20 minutes. Test for the gel stage, using the thermometer or plate test.

Remove from the heat. Skim off the foam, if necessary. Stir for 3–5 minutes to prevent floating fruit. Ladle into hot, sterilized jars, leaving 1/2 inch (1.2 cm) head space. Wipe the rims clean. Seal according to manufacturer's directions. Process the jars in a boiling water bath for 10 minutes.

Chunky Apple Marmalade with Ginger

Makes about 6 8-oz. (250-mL) jars

2	oranges	2
1	lemon	1
6 cups	peeled, chopped apples	1.5 L
1½ cups	water	360 mL
4½ cups	sugar	1.1 L
¼ cup	chopped candied ginger	60 mL

Brighten up an early-morning breakfast or a lazy Sunday brunch by serving this sprightly marmalade on hot toast, muffins or biscuits.

Cut the orange and lemon in half lengthwise, discarding the ends and seeds. Place the cut side down and slice the fruit very thinly. Cut the slices into small pieces (do not chop finely). Put the chopped fruit in a small pot and add just enough water to cover it. Simmer over medium heat for about 30 minutes, until the peel is tender. Drain, reserving the fruit. Prepare the preserving jars.

Combine the cooked orange and lemon, apples and water in your preserving pot. Bring to a boil over medium heat. Reduce the heat and simmer for about 10 minutes, until the apples are tender. Stir in the sugar and ginger. Increase the heat to medium and boil rapidly, stirring almost constantly, for 15–20 minutes, until thickened. Test for the gel stage, using the thermometer or plate test.

Remove from the heat. Skim off the foam if necessary. Stir for 3–5 minutes to prevent floating fruit. Ladle into hot, sterilized jars, leaving ½ inch (1.2 cm) head space. Wipe the rims clean. Seal according to manufacturer's directions. Process the jars in a boiling water bath for 10 minutes.

Facing page: *Marmalade Oatmeal Muffins (p.211).*

Previous page, from left to right: *Chunky Apple Marmalade with Ginger (p.75), Traditional English Marmalade (p.70), and Lemon-Lime Marmalade (p.72).*

Peach Orange Marmalade

Makes about 6 to 7 8-oz. (250-mL) jars

2	oranges	2
1	lemon	1
5 cups	finely chopped, unpeeled peaches	1.2 L
3½ cups	sugar	840 mL
½ tsp.	almond extract (optional)	2.5 mL

Prepare the preserving jars.

Grate the zest from the oranges and lemon. Place the zest in a small bowl and add enough boiling water to cover. Set aside.

Slice away as much of the white pith from the fruit as possible, preferably in large pieces. Chop the fruit very finely, reserving the seeds. Tie the seeds in a cheesecloth bag.

Drain the water from the zest. Combine the peaches, chopped oranges and lemon, zest, sugar and the cheesecloth bag in your preserving pot. Mix thoroughly.

Bring to a boil over medium heat. Boil rapidly, stirring often, for 25–30 minutes, until thickened. Test for the gel stage, using the thermometer or plate test.

Remove from the heat. Discard the cheesecloth bag, squeezing it out as much as possible. Skim off the foam if necessary. Stir for 3–5 minutes to prevent floating fruit. Stir in the almond extract, if desired. Pour into hot, sterilized jars, leaving ½ inch (1.2 cm) head space. Wipe the rims clean. Seal according to manufacturer's directions. Process the jars in a boiling water bath for 10 minutes.

Carrot Marmalade

Makes about 4 to 5 8-oz. (250-mL) jars

This bright orange marmalade is a natural served with poultry or game and equally good as a breakfast treat.

1	orange	1
1	lemon	1
4 cups	grated raw carrots	950 mL
3 cups	sugar	720 mL
1/2 tsp.	salt	2.5 mL

Using the coarse side of a box grater, grate the zest from the orange and lemon. Set the zest aside. Using a sharp knife, remove as much of the white pith as possible and discard. Cut the fruits in half, extract the juice and set aside. Chop the orange and lemon pulp into small pieces.

Combine the orange and lemon zest, juice and pulp in your preserving pot. Mix in the remaining ingredients. Let stand for 1 hour. Prepare the preserving jars.

Bring the mixture to a boil over medium heat, stirring occasionally. Simmer gently, stirring often, for 30 minutes, or until thickened. Test for the gel stage using the thermometer or plate test.

Remove from the heat. Skim off the foam if necessary. Stir for 3–5 minutes to prevent floating fruit. Pour the marmalade into hot, sterilized jars, leaving 1/2 inch (1.2 cm) head space. Wipe the rims clean. Seal according to manufacturer's directions. Process the jars in a boiling water bath for 10 minutes.

Pumpkin Marmalade

Makes about 4 to 5 8-oz. (250-mL) jars

A rather unusual marmalade with a thick, chunky texture and an excellent citrusy flavor.

1	orange	1
2	lemons	2
3 cups	water	720 mL
1	small pumpkin, about 3 lbs. (1.4 kg)	1
4 cups	sugar	950 mL

Cut the orange and lemons in half lengthwise. Place the cut side down and slice the fruit very thinly, discarding the ends. Cut the slices into small pieces (do not chop finely). Place the seeds in a cheesecloth bag.

In your preserving pot, combine the fruit, water and the bag of seeds. Bring to a boil over medium heat. Reduce the heat, cover and simmer until the fruit is tender, about 30 minutes. Remove the bag of seeds, squeeze it out well and discard.

While the fruit is cooking, prepare the pumpkin. Carefully cut the pumpkin in half and remove the seeds. Cut the pumpkin into chunks, then peel and cut away the stem ends. Dice the pumpkin into small pieces, about ½ inch (1.2 cm) square and ⅛ inch (.3 cm) thick. (Don't worry about being exact; these measurements are only to give you the approximate size.) You should end up with about 8 cups (2 L) of pumpkin. If you have extra, cook it up for dinner.

Add the sugar to the fruit mixture and cook over low heat, stirring until the sugar is dissolved, about 10 minutes. Prepare the preserving jars.

Add the 8 cups (2 L) of prepared pumpkin and increase the heat to medium-high. Cook rapidly, stirring often, for about 45–60 minutes, or until thickened. Test for the gel stage, using the thermometer or plate test.

Remove from the heat. Skim off the foam if necessary. Stir for 3 – 5 minutes to prevent floating fruit. Pour the marmalade into hot, sterilized jars, leaving ½ inch (1.2 cm) head space. Wipe the rims clean. Seal according to manufacturer's directions. Process the jars in a boiling water bath for 10 minutes.

Zany Zucchini Marmalade

Makes about 6 8-oz. (250-mL) jars

2	oranges	2
2	lemons	2
5 cups	grated zucchini (about 4 medium zucchini)	1.2 L
5 cups	sugar	1.2 L
2 Tbsp.	lemon juice	30 mL

Another in the never-ending search for new ways to use up extra zucchini… if only all vegetables grew as prolifically!

Prepare the preserving jars.

Slice the oranges and lemons thinly, discarding the ends and seeds. Chop very finely or process in a food processor until finely chopped, but not puréed.

Combine all the ingredients in your preserving pot. Bring to a boil over medium-high heat. Cook rapidly, stirring constantly, until the mixture thickens, about 20 – 25 minutes. Test for the gel stage, using the thermometer or plate test.

Remove from the heat. Skim off the foam if necessary. Stir for 3 – 5 minutes to prevent floating fruit. Pour the marmalade into hot, sterilized jars, leaving ½ inch (1.2 cm) head space. Wipe the rims clean. Seal according to manufacturer's directions. Process the jars in a boiling water bath for 10 minutes.

Winter Marmalade

Makes about 8 to 9 8-oz. (250-mL) jars

1 lb.	dried apricots	454 g
¼ lb.	dried cranberries	113 g
1	orange	1
1	14-oz. (398-mL) can of crushed pineapple	1
1	lemon, juice and finely grated zest	1
1½ cups	sugar	360 mL

Cut the apricots into small pieces with scissors. Place the apricots and cranberries in a bowl and pour boiling water over them, just enough to cover. Set aside to soak for at least 1 hour.

Drain the fruit, reserving ¾ cup (180 mL) of the liquid.

Slice the orange thinly, discarding the ends and seeds. Chop finely.

Prepare the preserving jars.

Combine all the ingredients, including the reserved soaking liquid, in your preserving pot. Bring to a boil over medium-high heat, stirring occasionally. Reduce the heat to medium and simmer, stirring often, for 45–60 minutes, or until thickened. Test for the gel stage, using the thermometer or plate test.

Remove from the heat. Skim off the foam if necessary. Stir for 3–5 minutes to prevent floating fruit. Ladle the marmalade into hot, sterilized jars, leaving ½ inch (1.2 cm) head space. Wipe the rims clean. Seal according to manufacturer's directions. Process the jars in a boiling water bath for 10 minutes.

Conserves

Conserves are essentially jams which have been dressed up by the addition of dried fruits and nuts. They are usually made from two or more fruits, often including a citrus fruit, and frequently contain spices or alcohol.

Conserves are very versatile. You can serve them as you would a jam, on morning toast or muffins, or offer them as imaginative toppings for desserts. A spicy, tart conserve can provide a distinctive contrast to salty dishes like ham, or a delicious foil to rich meats like roast pork, duck or goose.

The method for making conserves is exactly the same as the procedure for making jam. The fruit and sugar are boiled together until thickened but, unlike jams, nuts or alcohol or both are stirred into conserves during the final minutes of cooking. These ingredients do not require cooking and are added at the last minute so that the nuts will maintain their texture, and the alcohol its intense flavor. The alcohol in any conserve is always optional — leave it out if you like. Feel free to experiment with different combinations of dried fruits and nuts, substituting almonds for walnuts or prunes for raisins, according to your personal preference. Just keep the amounts the same.

About Cinnamon

Cinnamon is the dried bark of a tropical evergreen laurel tree. Closely related to another spice, cassia, the two are used interchangeably; in fact, cassia is often sold as cinnamon. Sweet and fragrant, cinnamon may be used to enhance a variety of preserves, from spiced jams to pickles. Cinnamon sticks may be added whole to flavor liquids, or broken and combined with other spices in a cheesecloth bag for easy removal. Ground cinnamon may be used in place of cinnamon sticks, but it may cause cloudiness in clear liquids. A universally popular spice, cinnamon is a component of spice mixtures from all over the world.

Grape Pecan Conserve

Makes about 5 8-oz. (250-mL) jars

2 lbs.	seedless green or red grapes	900 g
1	lemon	1
1	orange	1
3 cups	brown sugar	720 mL
1/4 cup	lemon juice	60 mL
1 cup	pecans, lightly toasted	240 mL
1/3 cup	brandy or rum (optional)	80 mL

Crunchy and sweet, this first-rate conserve makes a wonderful topping for toast or a luscious condiment with roast pork or chicken.

Stem the grapes and slice them in half. Cut the lemon and orange in quarters lengthwise, then slice thinly, discarding the ends and seeds.

In your preserving pot, combine the grapes, lemon and orange slices, sugar and lemon juice. Mix well, cover and let stand for 2–3 hours, to allow the juices to develop.

Prepare the preserving jars.

Bring the fruit and sugar mixture to a boil over medium heat and simmer, stirring often, for 45–60 minutes, until thickened. Test for gel if desired. Stir in the pecans. Cook 1 minute longer. Remove from the heat. Stir in the brandy or rum. Skim off the foam if necessary.

Ladle the conserve into hot, sterilized jars, leaving 1/2 inch (1.2 cm) head space. Wipe the rims clean. Seal according to manufacturer's directions. Process the jars in a boiling water bath for 10 minutes.

Papaya Nectarine Conserve

Makes 5 to 6 8-oz. (250-mL) jars

Chock-full of ripe, succulent fruit, this conserve is delectable served with scones for an old-fashioned afternoon tea.

4 cups	peeled, seeded, chopped papaya	950 mL
4 cups	pitted, chopped nectarines	950 mL
1/4 cup	lemon juice	60 mL
2 tsp.	finely grated lemon zest	10 mL
6 cups	sugar	1.5 L
1 cup	chopped dried apricots	240 mL
1/2 tsp.	nutmeg	2.5 mL

Prepare the preserving jars.

In your preserving pot, combine the papaya, nectarines, lemon juice and zest. Cover and simmer over medium heat for about 15 minutes, stirring occasionally, until the fruit is tender. Add the sugar, apricots and nutmeg, and cook another 15–20 minutes, until the mixture thickens, stirring often. Test for the gel stage if desired. Remove from the heat.

Ladle the conserve into hot, sterilized jars, leaving ½ inch (1.2 cm) head space. Wipe the rims clean. Seal according to manufacturer's directions. Process the jars in a boiling water bath for 10 minutes.

Plum Orange Conserve with Figs

Makes 5 to 6 8-oz. (250-mL) jars

Select firm, dark red or purple plums for this rich, elegant conserve. Make extra for Christmas gifts.

1	orange	1
6 cups	pitted, chopped plums	1.5 L
1/2 cup	orange juice	120 mL
3½ cups	brown sugar	840 mL
1 cup	chopped dried figs	240 mL
1 cup	chopped toasted walnuts	240 mL

Prepare the preserving jars.

Thinly slice the orange, discarding the ends and seeds. Chop very finely. Combine the orange, plums and orange juice in your preserving pot. Bring to a boil over medium heat. Simmer, stirring occasionally, until the plums are tender, about 15 minutes. Add the sugar and figs and cook another 15–20 minutes, until the conserve has thickened. Stir in the walnuts. Cook 1 minute longer. Remove from the heat.

Ladle the conserve into hot, sterilized jars, leaving ½ inch (1.2 cm) head space. Wipe the rims clean. Seal according to manufacturer's directions. Process the jars in a boiling water bath for 10 minutes.

About Toasting Nuts

Toasting nuts intensifies their flavor and will add a delicious new dimension to your conserves (and to other recipes too).

As toasted nuts become stale more quickly than raw nuts, you should only prepare the amount that you need for a single recipe.

To toast nuts in the oven, spread shelled nuts in a single layer on a baking sheet or cake pan and toast in a preheated 350°F (175°C) oven for 7–10 minutes, or until they are golden brown. Watch them carefully, stirring the nuts every couple of minutes, as the nuts around the perimeter will brown more quickly.

Always let toasted nuts cool completely before using.

To remove the skin from hazelnuts, transfer the nuts while still warm to a clean dish towel. Rub vigorously to remove most of the loose, papery skins.

To toast nuts in the microwave, spread the nuts in a microwave-safe dish, and microwave uncovered on high heat for 5–10 minutes, or until the nuts are golden brown. Cashews and Brazil nuts seem to brown more quickly than other types of nuts.

Spiced Pear, Peach and Citrus Conserve

Makes 5 to 6 8-oz. (250-mL) jars

Autumn is the ideal
time to make this
luscious conserve.
Choose fruit that is
ripe, but not too
soft or juicy.

1	3-inch (7.5-cm) broken cinnamon stick	1
½ tsp.	whole cloves	2.5 mL
2	lemons	2
1	orange	1
5	pears, peeled, cored and chopped	5
5	peaches, peeled, pitted and chopped	5
½ cup	orange juice	120 mL
4 cups	sugar	950 mL
1 cup	toasted slivered almonds	240 mL

Prepare the preserving jars. Put the cinnamon stick and cloves into a cheesecloth bag and tie the top with string.

Thinly slice the lemons and orange, discarding the ends and seeds. Chop very finely. Place in a small pot and add enough water to barely cover the fruit. Cover and simmer over low heat until the peel is very tender, about 20–30 minutes, adding additional water if necessary to keep the fruit moist. Drain and set aside.

Combine the pears, peaches and orange juice in your pre-serving pot. Cover and simmer over medium heat, stirring often, until the fruit is soft, about 10 minutes. Add the chopped lemon and orange, sugar and spice bag. Increase the heat to medium-high. Simmer, stirring often, for another 20–30 minutes, until the conserve has thickened. Test for the gel stage if desired. Stir in the almonds. Cook 1 minute longer. Remove from the heat. Discard the spice bag.

Ladle the conserve into hot, sterilized jars, leaving ½ inch (1.2 cm) head space. Wipe the rims clean. Seal according to manufacturer's directions. Process the jars in a boiling water bath for 10 minutes.

Cranberry, Rum and Raisin Conserve

Makes 6 to 7 8-oz. (250-mL) jars

2	oranges	2
3 cups	cranberries	720 mL
1 cup	cranberry or orange juice	240 mL
2 cups	brown sugar	475 mL
1 cup	dark raisins	240 mL
1 cup	coarsely chopped, toasted Brazil nuts	240 mL
½ cup	dark rum	120 mL

Prepare the preserving jars.

Slice the oranges thinly, discarding the ends and seeds. Chop very finely. Combine the orange, cranberries, cranberry or orange juice, brown sugar and raisins in your preserving pot. Bring to a boil over medium heat. Simmer, stirring often, for about 15 minutes, or until thickened. Stir in the Brazil nuts and rum and cook 1 minute longer. Remove from the heat.

Ladle the conserve into hot, sterilized jars, leaving ½ inch (1.2 cm) head space. Wipe the rims clean. Seal according to manufacturer's directions. Process the jars in a boiling water bath for 10 minutes.

Quick and simple to make, this conserve can also be made using frozen cranberries. No need to thaw them — just rinse and sort.

Preserves

The word "preserves" describes preserved foods as a group, but it also refers to a particular subgroup of preserved foods — a unique type of sweet spread, similar to jam, but requiring much more painstaking preparation. Preserves are a showcase for only the choicest fruit, making maximum use of its natural, juicy sweetness. Reserve your preserves for those occasions when you really want to make an impression, a show-off brunch, or a tea with your mother's friends. They are treasures to spoon up and savor with your most elegant "company's coming" desserts.

Preserves are made from whole, small fruits, like berries or cherries, or uniform pieces of larger fruits, like peaches or pears. The fruit for preserves is never crushed or chopped as it is for jam — the goal is to have identifiable pieces of fruit that retain their color, texture and shape. The chunks of fruit are tender and plump, suspended in a clear jelly-like syrup. The consistency of preserves is dependent on the amount of pectin present in the fruit; slightly underripe fruit is best.

Techniques for making preserves vary considerably, depending on the type of fruit that is being used. Soft fruits are usually layered with sugar for several hours, allowing their juices to develop. Layering is simply alternating layers of sugar and fruit in the pot; in effect, combining the two without stirring them. This helps to keep the fruit intact. Hard fruits — pears or apples, for example — are simmered in water or a sugar syrup to tenderize them and draw out their natural juices.

Preserves often take two to three days to prepare. One reason for this is the standing time, during which the juices are extracted. The other reason is that many types of preserves are

Facing page, foreground: *Spiced Pear, Peach and Citrus Conserve (p.86)*; background: *Cranberry, Rum and Raisin Conserve (p.87)*.

partially cooked, then poured into shallow dishes to encourage evaporation. During this process, the fruits steep in their syrup, absorbing sugar and becoming plump and juicy. This usually takes 12 to 24 hours.

As a result of these advance procedures, the final cooking time for preserves is reduced. The mixture is boiled rapidly for a brief period until the syrup thickens and the fruit appears translucent. The rapid cooking yields a fresh fruit flavor that is much more intense and concentrated than that of regular jams.

Facing page: *Classic Strawberry Preserves (p.93).*

This preserve is
delectable spooned
over ice cream or
cheesecake. Heavenly
with chocolate.

Sweet Cherry Preserves in Almond Syrup

Makes 6 to 7 8-oz. (250-mL) jars

8 cups	sweet firm cherries	2 L
6 cups	sugar	1.5 L
3 Tbsp.	lemon juice	45 mL
1 tsp.	almond extract	5 mL

Working over a bowl to catch the juice, pit the cherries and cut any extra-large ones in half.

Layer the cherries and sugar together in your preserving pot. Cover and let stand for 1–2 hours at room temperature, to draw out the juices.

Bring the mixture to a boil over low heat, stirring gently until the sugar is dissolved. Increase the heat to medium and boil for 10 minutes, shaking the pot occasionally or stirring very gently to prevent scorching. Remove from the heat. Stir in the lemon juice.

Pour the mixture into 1 or 2 shallow, heat-proof pans and let stand until cool. Cover loosely with cheesecloth or a dish towel and leave in a cool place for 12–18 hours or overnight.

The next day, prepare the preserving jars. Transfer the mixture to your preserving pot and bring to a boil over medium-high heat. Boil rapidly for 10 minutes, until slightly thickened. Stir gently or shake the pot often to prevent scorching.

Remove from the heat and skim off the foam if necessary. Add the almond extract, and stir for 5 minutes to prevent floating fruit. Ladle the preserves into hot, sterilized jars, leaving ½ inch (1.2 cm) head space. Wipe the rims clean. Seal according to manufacturer's directions. Process the jars in a boiling water bath for 10 minutes.

Classic Strawberry Preserves

Makes 5 to 6 8-oz. (250-mL) jars

6 cups	strawberries, about 3 – 3½ lbs. (1.4 – 1.6 kg)	1.5 L
5 cups	sugar	1.2 L
⅓ cup	lemon juice	80 mL

Hull the strawberries, but do not crush them. Layer the strawberries and sugar in your preserving pot. Cover and let stand at room temperature for 3 – 4 hours. Bring to a boil over low heat, stirring very gently until the sugar is dissolved. Increase the heat and boil rapidly for 15 minutes, stirring gently or shaking the pot often to prevent scorching. Stir in the lemon juice. Pour the mixture into 1 or 2 shallow, heat-proof pans. Let stand, uncovered, until cool. Cover with cheesecloth or a dish towel and leave in a cool place for 24 hours.

The next day, prepare the preserving jars. Return the mixture to your preserving pot and bring it quickly to a boil over medium-high heat. Boil rapidly for 10 – 15 minutes, shaking the pot or stirring gently to prevent scorching, until the syrup has thickened slightly.

Remove from the heat. Stir gently for about 5 minutes to prevent floating fruit. Skim off the foam if necessary. Ladle the preserves into hot, sterilized jars, leaving ½ inch (1.2 cm) head space. Wipe the rims clean. Seal according to manufacturer's directions. Process the jars in a boiling water bath for 10 minutes.

Don't be dismayed if your preserves end up syrupy instead of set — the pectin content of strawberries can vary tremendously. Strawberry preserves make a glorious dessert sauce. Select firm, slightly underripe (but not green!) strawberries, of uniform size, if possible.

Gingered Apple Preserves

Makes about 6 8-oz. (250-mL) jars

5 cups	sugar	1.2 L
2 cups	water	475 mL
1	3-inch (7.5 cm) cinnamon stick	1
8 cups	peeled, sliced apples, about 3 lbs. (1.4 kg), cut 1/4 inch (.6 cm) thick	2 L
3 Tbsp.	lemon juice	45 mL
1 Tbsp.	finely grated lemon zest	15 mL
1/2 – 3/4 cup	sliced preserved ginger in syrup	120 – 180 mL

Combine the sugar, water and cinnamon stick in your preserving pot. Bring to a boil over high heat, stirring often. Reduce the heat to medium, and simmer the mixture for 10 – 15 minutes. Prepare the preserving jars.

Toss the apple slices with the lemon juice and zest in a bowl. Drain the ginger, reserving the syrup, and slice thinly. Add the lemony apples, ginger and reserved syrup to the preserving pot. Simmer gently over medium heat for 35 – 40 minutes, until the syrup is slightly thickened and the apples appear translucent. Stir very gently or shake the pot often to prevent scorching.

Remove from the heat. Discard the cinnamon stick. Divide the apple slices equally among the hot, sterilized jars. Pour the syrup over to cover, leaving 1/2 inch (1.2 cm) head space. Wipe the rims clean. Seal according to manufacturer's directions. Process the jars in a boiling water bath for 10 minutes.

Plum Preserves with Orange Zest

Makes 5 to 6 8-oz. (250-mL) jars

Plum delicious! Damson or prune plums make the best preserves.

6 cups	halved, pitted firm plums, about 3 lbs. (1.4 kg)	1.5 L
½ cup	orange juice	120 mL
½ cup	water	120 mL
4½ cups	sugar	1.1 L
1 Tbsp.	grated orange zest	15 mL

Combine the plums and water in your preserving pot. Simmer gently over medium heat for 10 minutes. Using a slotted spoon, carefully remove the plums from the liquid and place them in a shallow, heat-proof pan. Add the sugar and orange zest to the liquid in the pot, bring to a boil over medium heat and simmer for 15 minutes, stirring occasionally. Remove from the heat and skim off the foam if necessary. Pour the syrup over the plums. Let stand uncovered until cool, then cover loosely with cheesecloth or a dish towel and let stand in a cool place for 12 – 18 hours or overnight.

The next day, prepare the preserving jars. Transfer the plums and syrup to your preserving pot and bring it to a boil over medium heat. Boil rapidly for 10–15 minutes until the mixture is slightly thickened. Stir gently or shake the pot often to prevent scorching.

Remove from the heat. Ladle the preserves into hot, sterilized jars, leaving ½ inch (1.2 cm) head space. Wipe the rims clean. Seal according to manufacturer's directions. Process the jars in a boiling water bath for 10 minutes.

Brandied Peach Preserves

Makes 5 to 6 8-oz. (250-mL) jars

A rich, intensely flavored preserve, accented with brandy. If you like, substitute apricots and Amaretto for the peaches and brandy. (Apricots do not need to be peeled.)

8 cups	peeled peaches (use mature, but underripe peaches), sliced about ½ inch (1.2 cm) thick	2 L
6 cups	sugar	1.5 L
½ cup	lemon juice	120 mL
½ cup	brandy	120 mL

In your preserving pot, layer the peaches and sugar together. Cover and let stand in a cool place overnight to draw out the juices.

The next day, bring the mixture to a boil over low heat, stirring gently until the sugar is dissolved. Increase the heat to medium and simmer for 10 minutes, shaking the pot occasionally or stirring gently to prevent scorching. Remove from the heat and stir in the lemon juice. Pour into 1 or 2 shallow, heat-proof pans and let stand until cool. Cover loosely with cheesecloth or a dish towel and leave in a cool place overnight.

The next day, prepare the preserving jars. Transfer the mixture to your preserving pot and bring it to a boil over medium-high heat. Boil rapidly for about 15 minutes, until the syrup has thickened slightly and the peaches look translucent. Stir gently or shake the pot often to prevent scorching.

Remove from the heat. Skim off the foam if necessary. Add the brandy and stir for 5 minutes to prevent floating fruit. Ladle the preserves into hot, sterilized jars, leaving ½ inch (1.2 cm) head space. Wipe the rims clean. Seal according to manufacturer's directions. Process the jars in a boiling water bath for 10 minutes.

Fruit Sauces

Preserved fruit sauces, sometimes referred to as compotes, are a wonderful staple to have on hand in the pantry — just waiting to enhance a variety of appetizers, main courses and desserts.

A fresh-tasting, tart fruit sauce is a lively companion to a veal pâté or chicken terrine. For the main course, pair a savory fruit sauce, such as Spiced Pear Sauce, with a crown roast of pork. Sauces with berries or cherries are a natural with chicken or duck.

Fruit sauces really shine at dessert time. Sweet fruit sauces can dress up any number of desserts, from simple ice cream, pound or angel food cake to an elegant trifle, cheesecake or dessert soufflé. Serve them spooned over poached fruit, rice pudding or gingerbread. You will no doubt find endless uses for these versatile toppings.

Simple concoctions of fruit, sugar and often juice or alcohol, fruit sauces are like a thinner version of jam, containing more fruit and less sugar.

Fruit sauces are simple to make. The fruit and sugar are simply simmered together until the fruit is cooked. Timing is not crucial and there is no need to test for a set. Then just pour the sauce into jars, process it and stash it away for a luscious taste of summer that you will enjoy year-round.

About Ginger

In its many forms, ginger is one of the most commonly used spices. Fresh ginger root (see page 161) has a strong, distinctive taste. Powdered ginger is the dried, ground root. Candied or crystallized ginger may be chopped and used in any number of sweet and savory preserves, from jams to chutneys; it is much less sharp-tasting than the fresh. Yet another form of ginger is stem ginger preserved in syrup — a very sweet, mild-flavored confection. Pickled ginger (preserved in vinegar) is a very popular condiment in Japan.

Pineapple, Strawberry and Rhubarb Dessert Sauce

Makes 7 to 8 8-oz. (250-mL) jars

A magical combination of three fruits that seem to have a natural affinity for each other.

7 cups	rhubarb, cut into ½-inch (1.2-cm) dice	1.7 L
2 cups	fresh pineapple, cut into ½-inch (1.2-cm) dice, or 1 19-oz. (532-mL) can drained pineapple tidbits	475 mL
2 cups	sliced strawberries	475 mL
¼ cup	lemon juice	60 mL
4 cups	sugar	950 mL

Prepare the preserving jars.

Combine the rhubarb, pineapple, strawberries and lemon juice in your preserving pot. Simmer over medium-low heat until the juices begin to form, then cover and simmer for 15 minutes, stirring often. Add the sugar, stirring to dissolve. Return the mixture to a boil and simmer, stirring often, for 20 minutes.

Remove from the heat. Stir 2–3 minutes and skim off the foam if necessary. Pour into hot, sterilized jars, leaving ½ inch (1.2 cm) head space. Wipe the rims clean. Seal according to manufacturer's directions. Process the jars in a boiling water bath for 10 minutes.

Honeyed Peach and Blueberry Compote

Makes about 6 to 7 8-oz. (250-mL) jars

This is a sensational sauce for a cheesecake or spooned over rich vanilla ice cream. Use fully ripe peaches.

5 cups	sliced, peeled peaches	1.2 L
5 cups	blueberries	1.2 L
1 cup	orange juice	240 mL
2 cups	sugar	475 mL
1 cup	honey	240 mL
1/3 cup	lemon juice	80 mL
1	3-inch (7.5-cm) cinnamon stick, broken in half	1

Prepare the preserving jars.

Combine the peaches, blueberries and orange juice in your preserving pot. Bring to a boil over medium heat. Cover and simmer for 10 minutes, stirring occasionally. Add the remaining ingredients, stirring until the sugar is dissolved. Return the mixture to a boil and simmer, stirring often, for 15–20 minutes, or until the sauce is slightly thickened.

Remove from the heat. Discard the cinnamon stick. Ladle the sauce into hot, sterilized jars, leaving ½ inch (1.2 cm) head space. Wipe the rims clean. Seal according to manufacturer's directions. Process the jars in a boiling water bath for 10 minutes.

Spirited Peach and Blueberry Compote. Add ¼ cup (60 mL) of peach schnapps or brandy before bottling.

Blackberry Orange Sauce with Port

Makes about 5 to 6 8-oz. (250-mL) jars

6 cups	blackberries	1.5 L
4 cups	sugar	950 mL
1 cup	orange juice	240 mL
¼ cup	lemon juice	60 mL
¼ cup	grated orange zest	60 mL
½ cup	port	120 mL

Don't go out and buy the most expensive port that you can find. (Save that for drinking!) Any moderately priced ruby port will do fine.

Prepare the preserving jars.

Combine the blackberries and sugar in your preserving pot and crush them with a potato masher. Add the orange and lemon juices and orange zest.

Bring to a boil over medium heat, then simmer for 20 minutes, stirring often. Remove from the heat and skim off the foam if necessary. Stir in the port.

Pour the sauce into hot, sterilized jars, leaving ½ inch (1.2 cm) head space. Wipe the rims clean. Seal according to manufacturer's directions. Process the jars in a boiling water bath for 10 minutes.

About Honey

Honey varies in color, aroma and flavor, depending on the type of flowers from which the bees have gathered the nectar. As a rule, the lighter the honey is in color, the milder the flavor will be. Clover honey, for example, is a delicate, light honey, while buckwheat honey is dark and strongly flavored.

Honey is sweeter than sugar, so when substituting honey for sugar, less honey is normally used.

Honey has a distinctive taste, which may mask more delicate flavors, so it is not suitable for use in all recipes.

Honey is so thick it is sometimes tricky to measure. Lightly grease your measuring cup or spoon so that the honey will come out more readily and use a rubber spatula to remove every last bit.

Spirited Cherry and Raspberry Compote

Makes about 5 to 6 8-oz. (250-mL) jars

This gorgeous dessert sauce partners exceptionally well with anything chocolate: chocolate mousse, chocolate terrine, even good old chocolate cake. Chambord is a raspberry liqueur made in France. Kirsch is made from cherries.

6 cups	tart cherries, pitted	1.5 L
3 cups	raspberries	720 mL
4 cups	sugar	950 mL
1/4 cup	lemon juice	60 mL
1/3 cup	Chambord liqueur, or kirsch	80 mL

Prepare the preserving jars.

Combine the cherries, raspberries and sugar in your preserving pot. Let stand for 15 minutes to allow the juices to develop. Stir in the lemon juice. Bring to a boil over medium heat. Simmer, stirring often, for 15–20 minutes, until slightly thickened.

Remove from the heat. Stir and skim off the foam if necessary. Stir in the Chambord liqueur. Pour the sauce into hot, sterilized jars, leaving 1/2 inch (1.2 cm) head space. Wipe the rims clean. Seal according to manufacturer's directions. Process the jars in a boiling water bath for 10 minutes.

About Pitting Cherries

When pitting cherries, always work over a bowl to catch the inevitable drops of cherry juice. Less juice will drip out if the cherries are chilled prior to pitting. Slit the cherries using a small, sharp knife, then use the tip of the knife to pop out the pit.

You may also use a cherry pitter — a handy, plunger-type gadget that pushes the pit right through the cherry, leaving only a small, neat hole. Cherry pitters are available in most cookware stores.

Spiced Pear Sauce

Makes about 5 to 6 8-oz. (250-mL) jars

8	large, juicy, ripe pears	8
3/4 cup	brown sugar, or more to taste	180 mL
2 Tbsp.	lemon juice	30 mL
1 1/2 tsp.	ginger	7.5 mL
1 tsp.	cinnamon	5 mL
1/2 tsp.	cloves	2.5 mL

Prepare the preserving jars. Peel, core and dice the pears.

Combine all the ingredients in your preserving pot. Bring to a boil over medium heat. Reduce the heat to low. Simmer, partially covered, for 20–25 minutes, or until the pears are soft. Stir occasionally.

Remove from the heat and mash vigorously with a potato masher until the mixture is fairly smooth. Return to a boil over medium-low heat, and cook for another 10 minutes, stirring constantly. Taste the pear sauce and add additional sugar, if necessary. Once the pear sauce is uniformly hot and bubbling, remove from the heat.

Spoon the sauce into hot, sterilized jars, leaving 1/2 inch (1.2 cm) head space. Wipe the rims clean. Seal according to manufacturer's directions. Process the jars in a boiling water bath for 10 minutes.

Absolutely divine served warm over homemade gingerbread, with a scoop of vanilla ice cream alongside.

Honeyed Applesauce

Makes about 5 to 6 pint (500-mL) jars

Experiment with different varieties of honey to lend a unique flavor to your applesauce. Applesauces can be made with any variety of apple, but the texture of the sauce may vary depending on the apple that is used. Some varieties of apples break down completely when cooked, while others tend to remain chunky.

6 lbs.	apples	2.7 kg
2 cups	apple juice or cider	475 mL
1 cup	water	240 mL
1/4 cup	lemon juice	60 mL
1/2 cup	honey, or to taste	120 mL
1 1/2 tsp.	cinnamon, or to taste	7.5 mL
	pinch of nutmeg	

Prepare the preserving jars. Peel and core the apples and cut into 1-inch (2.5-cm) chunks.

Combine apples, apple juice or cider, water and lemon juice in your preserving pot and bring to a boil over medium heat. Reduce the heat to medium-low, and simmer until the apples are very soft, 30–45 minutes, stirring often. Mash the apples thoroughly, using a potato masher. Stir in the honey and spices. Simmer for another 15 minutes, stirring constantly.

Remove from the heat. Ladle the applesauce into hot, sterilized jars, leaving 1/2 inch (1.2 cm) head space. Release the air bubbles if necessary. Wipe the rims clean. Seal according to manufacturer's directions. Process the jars in a boiling water bath for 20 minutes for either pints (500 mL) or quarts (1 L).

About Applesauce

Unquestionably the queen of fruit sauces, applesauce is terrific with everything from pancakes to pork chops. Mix it half and half with plain yogurt for a healthy treat, or bake it into muffins, cakes or quick breads. Applesauce is sensational spooned over baked squash, yams or sweet potatoes.

You can vary applesauce by mixing apples with other fruits. Pears, peaches and plums can lend an intriguing flavor to applesauce, and citrus juices and zests really punch up the taste. Berry applesauce can be made simply by adding cooked berry purée to your favorite homemade applesauce.

Fruit Butters

Fruit butters have a venerable tradition in the history of preserving. But until quite recently, they seemed to have fallen out of favor with home preservers, perhaps because they take a little extra time to prepare.

These old-fashioned favorites are now reappearing on pantry shelves, as we discover that fruit butters are among the most flavorful, versatile, and arguably, the most wholesome of homemade preserves.

Fruit butters are a tremendous way to utilize ripe or slightly overripe fruits that are not suitable for other types of preserves. Natural sugars are at their peak in such fruits, therefore very little extra sugar is needed, and the intense fruit flavors are concentrated.

And fear not, virtuous fruit butters contain no butter at all — the name simply refers to their smooth, velvety texture. They can be used *instead* of butter on your morning toast or muffins, for fewer than half the calories, and offer a change of pace from jams or jellies. For this reason, fruit butters are a more healthful choice for those who are monitoring fat, sugar or caloric intakes.

Fruit butters taste as good with meats and entrées as they do for breakfast and can be incorporated into sauces and baked goods as well.

Fruit butters require no special skills to make, but they are a little time-consuming. Plan to make fruit butter on a day when you have lots of time to spend in the kitchen, as it does demand a fair amount of attention. Perhaps you can have another project on the go and you can switch from one to the other to make the best use of your time.

Fruit butters are not as delicate as some preserves that require precise timing and careful balancing of pectin, acid and sugar. Butters don't actually gel, but thicken naturally during a long, slow cooking process — that gradually reduces the fruit pulp to a thick spreadable consistency.

Patience is a prerequisite, however, as it is essential to stir the butter almost constantly to prevent scorching, especially during the end of the cooking period.

But don't let this discourage you. If you persevere, you will be rewarded with a silky-smooth, naturally sweet, heavenly tasting ambrosia that will make all your efforts worthwhile.

How to Make Fruit Butters

Most traditional recipes for fruit butter were developed as a way to use up surplus fruit and therefore generally do not specify amounts.

Fruit butters, like jellies, are prepared in two steps — the first step readies the fruit for cooking in the second step. But this is where the similarities end.

Step 1: Preparing the Fruit Purée

▶ Place cut-up hard fruits or berries in your preserving pot. Hard fruits, such as apples or pears, should be cut into chunks, but do not need to be peeled.

▶ Add water or juice if using hard fruits.

▶ Crush the fruit if using soft berry-like fruits. No water is necessary as they will simmer in their own juice.

▶ Cover and simmer until the fruit is very soft, stirring often.

▶ For fruit with peels or pits, pass the fruit through a sieve or food mill. Soft fruits may be puréed in a blender or food processor.

Note: You can prepare fruit butter up to this point, then refrigerate the purée and continue with Step 2 later on.

Step 2: Cooking the Fruit Butter

▸ Measure the purée back into the preserving pot.

▸ Add the appropriate amount of sugar. Usually this will be one-third to half as much sugar as you have purée. If you are using honey instead of sugar, it is added later on in the cooking process, as the mixture reduces and starts to thicken.

▸ Stir over low heat to dissolve the sugar; continue to simmer the butter over low heat until it is very thick.

▸ Stir the butter almost constantly to prevent scorching; this is especially important once it begins to thicken. Use a long-handled spoon, as fruit butters tend to spatter.

▸ Towards the end of the cooking time, once the butter has thickened somewhat, add the spices. This is also the time to add honey if you are using it.

▸ To determine if the butter is ready, draw your spoon through the center of the butter, making a trough. If the trough doesn't immediately fill with liquid, the butter is done. You can also test by dropping a teaspoonful of butter onto a chilled plate. If no juice oozes away from the more solid mass of the butter, it is ready to be put into jars.

▸ Can the butter as you would any other type of sweet preserve, although due to its thickness it is usually best to spoon the butter into the jars. Butters tend to trap air bubbles because of their density, so be sure to release any pockets of air by running a non-metal utensil around the inside of the glass.

▸ Process the jars of butter in a boiling water bath, as directed in the recipe.

Wild Blackberry Butter

Makes 6 to 7 8-oz. (250-mL) jars

8 cups	blackberries	2 L
6	large apples, about 2 lbs. (900 g)	6
	sugar	
½ tsp.	cloves	2.5 mL
½ tsp.	cinnamon	2.5 mL

Blackberries are free for the picking along many roadsides or in deserted lots. Use fully ripe, juicy berries for this butter.

Place the blackberries in your preserving pot and crush them with a potato masher. Core the apples and chop them coarsely. Add the apples to the blackberries.

Bring to a boil over medium-low heat. Cover and simmer for about 30 minutes, or until the apples are soft, stirring often. Remove from the heat and pass the mixture through a sieve or food mill.

Prepare the preserving jars.

Measure the purée back into the preserving pot and add ½–¾ cup (120–180 mL) of sugar for each cup of purée. Taste as you add the sugar: the amount will depend on your own personal preference as well as the sweetness or tartness of the berries.

Stir well to dissolve the sugar and simmer over low heat, stirring often, for 45–60 minutes. Once the butter starts to get quite thick, towards the end of the cooking time, add the spices. Stir constantly from this point on to prevent scorching. Test for doneness if desired.

Remove from the heat. Spoon the butter into hot, sterilized jars, leaving ½ inch (1.2 cm) head space. Release the air bubbles. Wipe the rims clean. Seal according to manufacturer's directions. Process the jars in a boiling water bath for 10 minutes.

Apple Butter

Makes 6 to 7 8-oz. (250-mL) jars

5 lbs.	tart apples	2.25 kg
2 cups	apple juice or cider	475 mL
1½–2 cups	brown sugar	360 – 475 mL
2 Tbsp.	lemon juice	30 mL
1 Tbsp.	cinnamon	15 mL
½ tsp.	each cloves, allspice and nutmeg	2.5 mL

Core the apples and chop them coarsely. Combine the apples and apple juice or cider in your preserving pot. Bring to a boil over medium heat. Reduce the heat to low, cover and simmer for about 20 minutes, or until the apples are tender. Stir occasionally. Remove from the heat. Pass the mixture through a sieve or food mill.

Measure the purée back into your preserving pot. Add ½ – ⅔ cup (120–160 mL) of sugar for each cup of purée, depending on the tartness of the apples. Add the lemon juice and mix well. Cook over low heat, stirring almost constantly, for 35 – 45 minutes, or until thickened. Stir in the spices during the last 10 – 15 minutes of the cooking time. Test for doneness if desired.

Remove from the heat. Spoon the butter into hot, sterilized jars, leaving ½ inch (1.2 cm) head space. Release the air bubbles. Wipe the rims clean. Seal according to manufacturer's directions. Process the jars in a boiling water bath for 10 minutes.

Pear Orange Butter

Makes 5 to 6 8-oz. (250-mL) jars

A sweet, silky butter subtly spiked with orange and ginger.

4 lbs.	ripe, juicy pears	1.8 kg
1 cup	orange juice	240 mL
3 Tbsp.	lemon juice	45 mL
2 cups	sugar (or to taste)	475 mL
½ tsp.	ginger	2.5 mL

Core the pears and chop them coarsely. Combine the pears, orange juice and lemon juice in your preserving pot and bring to a boil over medium heat. Reduce the heat to low. Cover and simmer for about 30 minutes, until the pears are very soft, stirring occasionally. Remove from the heat and pass the mixture through a sieve or food mill.

Prepare the preserving jars.

Return the purée to the pot and add the sugar, stirring until it is dissolved. Simmer over medium-low heat, stirring almost constantly, for 40–50 minutes, or until the butter is very thick. Stir in the ginger during the last 10–15 minutes of the cooking time. Test for doneness if desired.

Remove from the heat. Spoon the butter into hot, sterilized jars, leaving ½ inch (1.2 cm) head space. Release the air bubbles. Wipe the rims clean. Seal according to manufacturer's directions. Process the jars in a boiling water bath for 10 minutes.

Using Honey in Fruit Butters

You may prefer to use honey instead of sugar to sweeten fruit butters. Remember that all honeys have a definite flavor, and will impart that to your butter. For this reason, a mild, light-colored honey is the best choice.

You will need much less honey than sugar, usually about half the amount. The honey is added near the end of the cooking time, at the same time that you add the spices. Simply taste the fruit mixture and add enough honey to sweeten it to your liking.

This butter is much less
time-consuming than
most. Cranberries are
full of pectin, causing
the butter to thicken
up quickly.

Quick Cranberry Butter

Makes 6 to 7 8-oz. (250-mL) jars

10 cups	cranberries	2.4 L
1½ cups	cranberry juice	360 mL
1½ cups	honey or maple syrup (or to taste)	360 mL
½ tsp.	allspice	2.5 mL

Combine the cranberries and juice in your preserving pot. Cover and cook over medium-low heat until the cranberries are soft, about 20–30 minutes, stirring occasionally. Cool the mixture slightly, then purée it in a blender or food processor until smooth.

Prepare the preserving jars.

Return the cranberry purée to the preserving pot and add the honey or maple syrup and allspice. Simmer over low heat, stirring constantly, about 15–20 minutes, until the butter is thick. Test for doneness.

Remove from the heat. Spoon the butter into hot, sterilized jars, leaving ½ inch (1.2 cm) head space. Release the air bubbles. Wipe the rims clean. Seal according to manufacturer's directions. Process the jars in a boiling water bath for 10 minutes.

Cooking Fruit Butters in the Oven

Fruit butters may also be cooked in the oven and many cooks prefer this method. It requires less stirring and tends to be less messy.

You still have to prepare the fruit purée in a pot on top of the stove (Step 1). The difference is in Step 2.

A preserving pot is not suitable for cooking fruit butters in the oven. Use a large, shallow roasting pan made of stainless steel, glass or enamel-coated metal. It is important to have the maximum surface area of the butter exposed to the heat to encourage evaporation. Cook the butter, uncovered, at 325 °F (165 °C) until thick, stirring occasionally.

Plum Butter

Makes 5 to 6 8-oz. (250-mL) jars

12 cups	coarsely chopped, pitted plums	3 L
1 cup	water	240 mL
4 cups	sugar (or to taste)	950 mL
1/2 tsp.	cinnamon	2.5 mL
1/2 tsp.	cloves	2.5 mL

Combine the plums and water in your preserving pot. Cover and simmer over medium heat for about 20 minutes, or until the plums are tender. Stir occasionally. Remove from the heat. Pass the mixture through a sieve or food mill (or if you don't mind the barely discernible bits of skin, purée in a food processor).

Prepare the preserving jars.

Return the purée to the preserving pot. Stir in the sugar until it is dissolved. Simmer over medium-low heat, stirring almost constantly, for 30–40 minutes, or until the mixture is somewhat thickened. Stir in the spices during the last 10–15 minutes of the cooking time. Test for doneness if desired.

Remove from the heat. Spoon the butter into hot, sterilized jars, leaving 1/2 inch (1.2 cm) head space. Release the air bubbles. Wipe the rims clean. Seal according to manufacturer's directions. Process the jars in a boiling water bath for 10 minutes.

Serve this mellow, richly flavored butter with roast pork or turkey, or as a spread on fruit or nut quick breads.

Peach, Mango, Nectarine or Papaya Butter

Makes 7 to 8 8-oz. (250-mL) jars

Only ripe, juicy, succulent fruits will do for this recipe. I like to use lemon juice with peaches or nectarines and lime juice with mangos and papayas. Pure ambrosia!

10 cups	chopped, peeled fruit	2.4 L
2/3 cup	orange juice	160 mL
1/3 cup	lemon or lime juice	80 mL
2 cups	sugar (or to taste)	475 mL
1/2 tsp.	ginger	2.5 mL
1/2 tsp.	nutmeg	2.5 mL

Combine the fruit, orange juice and lemon or lime juice in your preserving pot. Bring to a boil over medium heat. Reduce the heat to low, cover and simmer for about 20 minutes, or until the fruit is very soft. Stir often. Remove from the heat. Cool the mixture slightly, then purée it in a blender or food processor until smooth.

Prepare the preserving jars.

Return the purée to the preserving pot and stir in the sugar. Simmer over medium-low heat, stirring almost constantly, for 35–40 minutes, until thickened. Add the spices during the last 10–15 minutes of the cooking time. Test for doneness, if desired.

Remove from the heat. Spoon the butter into hot, sterilized jars, leaving 1/2 inch (1.2 cm) head space. Release the air bubbles. Wipe the rims clean. Seal according to manufacturer's directions. Process the jars in a boiling water bath for 10 minutes.

Pickles

Many people who have never tried their hand at pickling are astonished how simply and quickly many varieties of pickles can be made. It is possible to complete a batch of pickles in an afternoon, and then reap the mouth-watering benefits for weeks and months to come.

Pickling, the preservation of vegetables or fruits in a vinegar and/or salt solution, is one of the most ancient methods of preserving foods.

There are three basic forms of pickling: long-term brining, short-term brining and quick process (also known as fresh-pack).

The traditional long-term brining process, utilizing controlled fermentation, can take weeks or months to accomplish and requires close supervision. In this method, vegetables are placed into a large crock and covered with a saltwater solution, the brine. As fermentation occurs, lactic acid is produced, increasing the acidity of the solution and controlling the growth of undesirable microorganisms.

Pickles produced by this age-old, natural process have a characteristic, sharp, tangy flavor. Only certain types of vegetables are suitable for fermentation pickling.

A second method, short-term or non-fermentation brining, is a two-step process which involves submerging vegetables in a high salt or salt-vinegar brine for several hours or days, desalting them, then bottling them in a vinegar pickling liquid.

The main disadvantages of both brining methods are that they are time- and space-consuming.

The recipes here use a speedier, more straightforward procedure called the fresh-pack method. Most modern pickle recipes use this method and it is more appropriate for small quantities.

Some purists argue that fermentation produces a distinct flavor that cannot be duplicated by fresh-packing in vinegar. This may be so, but fresh-packing, done properly, provides the most thorough protection from spoilage. This, combined with the ease and convenience of fresh-packing, makes it the method of choice for most picklers today.

In fresh-packing, vinegar provides the acid necessary to prevent spoilage. It is important to note that you must always follow pickle recipes exactly. Never reduce the amount of vinegar called for in a recipe. If you find a particular pickle too tangy, add a little sugar the next time to offset its tartness, or simply find another recipe that is more suited to your taste.

Many types of pickles made by the fresh-pack method can be completed within an hour or two. In some recipes, the clean vegetables or fruit are simply placed directly into the jars, salt and seasonings added and a hot vinegar solution poured over the food to cover it. Other recipes may call for steeping or simmering the produce in a vinegar solution, while others require short-brining foods with salt for a few hours or overnight. The pickles are then briefly processed in a boiling water bath.

Despite what you may have read or heard, for safety's sake, all pickles must be heat processed, as directed in the recipe. This ensures that any organisms that might cause spoilage have been destroyed. In addition, heat processing is the final step that provides your jars with an airtight seal. Heat processing, if done correctly, will not cause pickles to become soft. As long as top-quality produce is used in properly balanced, well-tested recipes and recommended processing times are followed, you will achieve a superior crisp result.

Virtually any vegetable and many fruits can be pickled successfully, but obviously some will make better pickles than others. Making your own pickles can be a highly personal experience — you can vary spices, herbs and seasonings to suit your own individual taste. No wonder so many old-time pickle recipes are named after their makers! This chapter includes a wide variety of pickles to appeal to many different tastes — I hope that they will inspire you to become an enthusiastic and passionate pickler.

The Essentials of Making Pickles

Vegetables and Fruits

As always, select the finest and freshest vegetables and fruits available. Produce intended for pickling should not be more than 24 hours old — this is especially important with cucumbers, which tend to deteriorate quickly after picking. Choose young, tender vegetables and firm, ripe fruits. Never use any bruised, moldy or overripe produce for pickling — nothing can spoil a batch of pickles faster. Imperfect specimens may be saved for relishes or chutneys as long as the undesirable parts are cut away and discarded.

All foods must be washed thoroughly, in some cases vigorously scrubbed with a vegetable brush, to remove dirt. Rinse in clear water and pat dry.

Vinegar

Use vinegar that contains at least 5 percent acetic acid. This is pretty much any type of vinegar, except homemade. You may find a special pickling vinegar with a 7 percent acidity level. It will give a more astringent flavor and possibly a crisper texture to pickles.

Handling Hot Peppers

Hot peppers must be handled with caution. They release fumes and oils that can cause excruciating pain to the sensitive tissues of your eyes, nose, lips, even your fingertips, especially if you have any cuts or abrasions. The alkaloid capsaicin that is present in hot peppers is used as the active ingredient in pepper spray, a product designed to ward off muggers. The white membrane inside the pepper, holding the seeds, is the hottest part.

Always wear rubber gloves when handling hot peppers. Medical-type latex gloves are great, because you can throw them out when you're finished, but regular rubber gloves are fine too. Just be sure to wash them carefully after each use to remove any remaining oils. And don't forget to wash utensils you have used as well.

The choice of vinegar really depends on the flavor that you want, although color does play an important part. Cider vinegar, for example, imparts a mellow flavor but will discolor pale vegetables such as cauliflower or onions. Red wine vinegar does likewise. Only white wine or white distilled vinegar will not affect the color of your pickles.

Sugar

Use white granulated sugar for pickling, unless the recipe specifically calls for brown. Brown sugar tends to darken pickles. An exception would be in pickled beets or onions, where a particular flavor, not color, is the issue. Brown sugar is also commonly used in chutneys and relishes.

Water

Soft water makes the best pickles. Minerals present in hard water may cause pickles to darken or become soft. To soften hard tap water, simply boil it for 15 minutes, then let it stand, covered, for 24 hours. Carefully skim off any scum that has formed on the surface, then pour it slowly out of the container without disturbing any sediment. An easier but more expensive alternative is to buy distilled water.

Salt

Use coarse pickling salt only. Regular table salt contains iodine and anti-caking agents that may darken or cloud pickling liquids. Sea salt contains minerals that may cause discoloration of light-colored foods. Kosher salt is a pure, but somewhat weak relative of pickling salt and is difficult to measure.

Seasonings

Herbs and spices add immeasurably to the flavor of your finished product. For finest quality and taste, always use fresh seasonings. Spices that have been stored too long tend to deteriorate and lose their pungency. It is a good idea to purchase new spices at the start of each pickling season. Buy small quantities and store them away from heat in airtight containers.

Either fresh or dried herbs may be used in pickling, but try to avoid powdered seasonings that tend to darken or cloud pickling liquids. Whole spices may be added loose to boiling pickling liquids, then strained out, or a spice bag may be used for easy removal. Sometimes whole spices are placed directly into the jars and left there to add to the visual appeal of the pickles.

Pickle Problems

Because so many factors can affect the pickling process, things may occasionally go wrong. If you have any doubts about the quality of your pickles, it is essential to determine if they are safe to eat, or if the pickles are potentially hazardous and must be discarded.

The following are signs that pickles are unsafe to eat. If any of these signs are present, THROW THE PICKLES OUT. Never taste a questionable food as a test for spoilage. Destroy the food so it cannot be eaten by people or animals.

- ▶ A broken seal or a bulging or leaking lid.
- ▶ Mold in the contents of the jar, around the rim or on the underside of the lid.
- ▶ Pressure inside the jar or liquid that spurts from the jar upon opening.
- ▶ Fermentation, gassiness or bubbles in the contents.

- Sour, yeasty or off odors—any kind of unpleasant or musty smell.

- Slimy, mushy or slippery pickles.

Sometimes pickles may not be absolutely perfect, but they are still safe to eat. Here are some examples.

- Pickles are not crisp and crunchy. (There was not enough salt or vinegar in the recipe.)

- Pickles look bleached or pale. (They were exposed to too much light during storage.)

- Pickles are shriveled. (Cooked pickles were heated too vigorously in a vinegar/sugar solution, the vinegar or salt solution was too strong, the vegetables were not fresh enough or hard water was used.)

- Pickles are hollow. (Raw cucumbers were either poorly developed or too mature, or raw cucumbers were the wrong variety or stored too long before use.)

- Pickles are dark or murky-looking. (Too many spices—or ground spices—were added; iodized table salt was used instead of pickling salt; iron, copper, brass or zinc utensils or cookware were used; a dark vinegar was used; hard water was used; cooked pickles were heated too long.)

- Garlic turns green or blue. (Although unappetizing, this color change is just the result of a chemical reaction and is harmless. It may occur if the garlic is immature, or not fully dry. It may help to blanch the garlic in boiling water before use.)

- Cauliflower or onions turn pink. (Colorless pigments that are naturally present in these foods change color in the presence of an acid — vinegar. As with garlic, this reflects a chemical change and is nothing to worry about.)

Pickle Pointers

- ▸ Read and follow the advice regarding the selection of produce, ingredients and utensils.

- ▸ Use reliable, up-to-date pickle recipes.

- ▸ Don't start pickling until you have thoroughly read the recipe, assembled all the ingredients, and have your produce prepared and your equipment ready to go.

- ▸ Work quickly and follow instructions. Both the jars and the pickling liquid must be good and hot or the pickles may not seal properly. It is especially important to heed recommendations that direct you to pack jars one at a time. Packing food in jars can be time-consuming and this method ensures that everything stays hot.

- ▸ Don't try to make large batches of pickles. Your pickling adventure will be more successful and enjoyable if you make pickles in small, manageable amounts. You can always make more!

- ▸ It is advisable to wait several weeks at least before testing pickles to allow the flavors time to develop and mingle.

About Pickling Spice

Indispensable in the flavoring of — guess what?— pickles, pickling spice originated in England. It is a mixture of several whole spices, including cinnamon, bay leaves, peppercorns, mustard seed, mace, cloves, dill seed, chili pepper, coriander seed and allspice. You can certainly blend your own if you like, but pickling spice is easy to find. Pickling spice may either be tied into a cheesecloth bag and removed once pickling is completed or placed loose in the jars of pickles to add flavor and visual appeal.

Simply Good Dill Pickles

Makes 4 quart (1-L) jars

4 lbs.	pickling cucumbers	1.8 kg
4 cups	water	950 mL
3 cups	vinegar	720 mL
12	heads fresh dill, plus some leaves	12
8	cloves garlic, peeled (optional)	8
8	small hot chili peppers (optional)	8
4 Tbsp.	pickling salt	60 mL
4 tsp.	mixed pickling spice	20 mL

Scrub the cucumbers thoroughly. Cut a ¼-inch (.6-cm) slice from the blossom end. Slice if necessary (see "About Cucumbers," page 125). Prepare the preserving jars.

Combine the water and vinegar in your preserving pot and bring to a boil. Reduce heat and keep at a simmer.

Working with one jar at a time, place 3 dill heads (and some leaves), 2 garlic cloves, 2 hot peppers, 1 Tbsp. (15 mL) salt and 1 tsp. (5 mL) pickling spice in each jar.

Fill the hot, sterilized jar with cucumbers to within 1 inch (2.5 cm) of the rim, wedging them in so that none can escape and float to the top when the liquid is added. Pour in the hot vinegar solution, leaving ½ inch (1.2 cm) head space. Release the air bubbles. Top up with liquid, leaving ¼ inch (.6 cm) head space. Wipe the rims clean. Seal according to manufacturer's directions. Repeat with the remaining jars. Process the jars in a boiling water bath for 15 minutes.

Previous page, from left to right: *Pickled Grapes with Tarragon (p.133) Pickled Asparagus (p.128), Michael's Pickled Onions (p. 132).*

Facing page, from left to right: *Pickled Rosemary Carrots (p.127), Simply Good Dill Pickles (p. 123), Striped Pickled Peppers (p. 126).*

Crisp and tangy, these pickles can be garlicky or not, spicy or not, to suit your own taste. But be sure to use plenty of nice, fresh dill — both the heads and leaves.

To add an unusual flavor to homemade salad dressing, substitute some strained, leftover pickle juice for part of the vinegar in your recipe.

Authentic Bread and Butter Pickles

Makes about 5 to 6 pint (500-mL) jars

This classic pickle is a favorite with sliced cold meats and cheeses or any savory sandwich.

All cucumbers are not created equal. Long English cucumbers, while superior for eating raw, are not suitable for pickling. Neither are waxed cucumbers from the supermarket; the waxy coating that is used to prolong their shelf life cannot be penetrated by a pickling solution. (However, they may be peeled and used for relishes.)

4 lbs.	medium, unwaxed cucumbers (about 6–8), unpeeled, cut into ⅛-inch (.3-cm) slices	1.8 kg
4	onions, peeled, halved and cut into ⅛-inch (.3-cm) slices	4
2	red bell peppers, cored, seeded, halved and cut into ⅛-inch (.3-cm) slices	2
⅓ cup	pickling salt	80 mL
4 cups	white vinegar	950 mL
3 cups	sugar	720 mL
2 tsp.	celery seed	10 mL
2 tsp.	mustard seed	10 mL
1 tsp.	ginger	5 mL
1 tsp.	turmeric	5 mL

Discard the stem and blossom ends of the cucumbers. Combine the prepared vegetables and salt in a large bowl. Cover with ice water. Chill overnight.

The next day, drain the vegetables in a colander. Rinse well. Prepare the preserving jars.

Combine the remaining ingredients in your preserving pot. Bring to a boil over high heat. Add the vegetables and return to a boil. Cook briefly, about 1 minute, or just until the cucumbers change color.

Using a slotted spoon, ladle the pickles into the hot, sterilized jars. Fill the jars up with liquid to within ½ inch (1.2 cm) of the rim. Make sure that the liquid covers all the pickle slices. Release the air bubbles. Wipe the rims clean. Seal according to manufacturer's directions. Process the jars in a boiling water bath for 10 minutes.

Pickled Garlic

Makes about 4 8-oz. (250-mL) jars

2 cups	garlic cloves, about 1½ lbs. (680 g)	475 mL
3 cups	red or white wine vinegar	720 mL
¼ cup	pickling spice	60 mL
2 tsp.	pickling salt	10 mL

Fill a medium-sized pot with water and bring to a boil over high heat. Add the garlic, stir and simmer for 1 minute. Remove from the heat. Drain the garlic in a colander and rinse in cold water. Slip the skins off the garlic. Set aside.

Prepare the preserving jars.

Combine the remaining ingredients in your preserving pot and bring to a boil over high heat. Turn the heat down, cover and keep hot. Pack the garlic into hot, sterilized jars, leaving ½ inch (1.2 cm) head space. Pour the hot vinegar solution over the garlic cloves, leaving ¼ inch (.6 cm) head space. Release the air bubbles. Wipe the rims clean. Seal according to manufacturer's directions. Process the jars in a boiling water bath for 5 minutes.

A real hit at Halloween parties, pickled garlic may be served alongside traditional pickles as a snack or finely chopped to enliven salad dressings or sauces. Use narrow-mouthed preserving jars for these pickles.

About Alum

A fine white powder used in old-time recipes as an aid in keeping pickles crisp. Alum may cause bitterness in pickles, and is no longer recommended as it may cause stomach upset in some people.

Striped Pickled Peppers

Makes about 5 pint (500-mL) jars

4 cups	white vinegar	950 mL
2 cups	water	475 mL
4	medium-sized yellow bell peppers, about 2 lbs. (900 g) in total, seeded, cored and cut lengthwise in ½-inch (1.2-cm) strips	4
4	medium-sized red bell peppers, about 2 lbs. (900 g) in total, seeded, cored and cut lengthwise in ½-inch (1.2-cm) strips	4
5	cloves garlic, peeled	5
5 tsp.	pickling salt	25 mL
2½ tsp.	sugar	12.5 mL

Prepare the preserving jars.

Combine the vinegar and water in your preserving pot and bring to a boil. Reduce heat and keep at a simmer.

Working with one jar at a time, place 1 clove garlic, 1 tsp. (5 mL) salt and ½ tsp. (2.5 mL) sugar in each jar. Arrange the pepper strips upright in the jar, packing them tightly and alternating red and yellow. Place the most attractive, uniform slices around the perimeter; the shorter peppers can go in the center. Sometimes it helps to place the jar on its side.

Pour the hot vinegar solution over the peppers, leaving ½ inch (1.2 cm) head space. Release the trapped air bubbles. Add additional liquid if necessary, leaving ¼ inch (.6 cm) head space. Wipe the rims clean. Seal according to manufacturer's directions. Repeat with the remaining jars. Process the jars in a boiling water bath for 10 minutes.

Pickled Rosemary Carrots

Makes 5 to 6 pint (500-mL) jars

3 cups	water	720 mL
3 cups	vinegar	720 mL
¼ cup	each sugar and pickling salt	60 mL
2 Tbsp.	mixed peppercorns	30 mL
6	cloves garlic, peeled	6
6	small hot chili peppers, preferably red	6
4 lbs.	carrots, peeled, cut into sticks 4 inches (10 cm) long about and ½ inch (1.2 cm) wide	1.8 kg
6	3-inch (7.5-cm) sprigs fresh rosemary	6

Prepare the preserving jars. Combine the water, vinegar, sugar, salt and peppercorns in your preserving pot. Bring to a boil over high heat. Reduce the heat to medium and simmer for 5 minutes.

Working with one jar at a time, place 1 clove of garlic and 1 chili pepper in each hot, sterilized jar. Pack the carrot sticks tightly into the jar, standing them upright. Slide one sprig of rosemary into the jar. Carefully pour the boiling vinegar solution into the jars, leaving ¼ inch (.6 cm) head space. Release the air bubbles. Wipe the rims clean. Seal according to manufacturer's directions. Repeat with the remaining jars. Process the jars in a boiling water bath for 15 minutes.

Carrots are a wonderful addition to your pickle pantry. Their vivid orange color provides a delightful contrast to all that green! Don't attempt these pickles unless you have fresh rosemary—dried rosemary won't do.

Mixed peppercorns are a colorful blend of whole black, white, green and pink peppercorns. If you can't find them, black peppercorns are just fine.

About Cucumbers

When pickling, cucumbers up to 4 inches (10 cm) long may be used whole, while longer cucumbers, as long as they are firm, can be halved, quartered or sliced. Freshly harvested cucumbers are a must, as older specimens may become shrivelled after pickling. Sometimes pickling cucumbers start out hollow. Hollow cucumbers will usually float in water—weed them out while you're washing your cukes and save them for relish. Make sure to cut a ⅛- to ¼-inch (.3- to .6-cm) slice from the blossom end of pickling cucumbers. These blossoms contain an enzyme that can cause pickles to soften.

Pickled Asparagus

Makes about 3 quart (1-L) jars

5–6 lbs.	asparagus	2.25–2.75 kg
3 cups	water	720 mL
3 cups	white vinegar	720 mL
2	small onions, peeled, halved and cut into ¼-inch (.6-cm) slices	2
6	cloves garlic, peeled	6
3	small hot chili peppers (optional)	3
3 Tbsp.	pickling salt	45 mL
3 Tbsp.	vinegar	45 mL
3 Tbsp.	mustard seeds	45 mL
2 Tbsp.	dill seeds	30 mL

To most of us, the first asparagus is truly a sign of the onset of spring. When you have eaten your fill of fresh asparagus, pickle some to enjoy later on in the year. Asparagus deteriorates quickly, so be sure to preserve it as soon as possible once you get it home. Select firm, straight asparagus with closed dry tips. Try to choose spears that are about the same thickness — ½ inch (1.2 cm) in diameter is best.

Prepare the asparagus spears. Trim the spears to jar length. They should stand about 1 inch (2.5 cm) shorter than the rim of the jar. Measure carefully ahead of time as it can be very frustrating to be trimming asparagus as you are trying to pack them into the jars.

You will find that you are cutting off a heart-breaking amount of tender asparagus along with the tough ends. Save the trimmings to make Pickled Asparabits or to use in soups, salads or stir-fries.

Prepare the preserving jars.

Combine the water and vinegar in your preserving pot and bring to a boil. Reduce the heat to keep the liquid at a simmer.

Working with one jar at a time, place a third of the onion slices, 2 cloves of garlic, 1 chili pepper, 1 Tbsp. (15 mL) each of salt, sugar and mustard seeds, and 2 tsp. (10 mL) of dill seeds in each jar. Pack the asparagus into the jar, tips down. It helps to lay the jar on its side, and pack the asparagus first around the perimeter of the jar, then fill in the center. The asparagus must be packed in quite tightly.

Carefully pour the hot vinegar solution into the jars, leaving ¼ inch (.6 cm) head space. Release the air bubbles. Add additional liquid if necessary. Wipe the rims clean. Seal according to manufacturer's directions. Repeat with the remaining jars. Process the jars in a boiling water bath for 20 minutes.

Pickled Asparabits

Use only the tender asparagus trimmings, cut into small pieces no longer than 1 inch (2.5 cm) long. The "bits" need not be in uniform pieces. Use pint (500-mL) jars. Narrow-mouthed jars are best. Prepare the jars and make up a batch of pickling liquid using equal amounts of vinegar and water. You may even have a little liquid left over from the Pickled Asparagus. Heat the liquid to a simmer.

To each jar add:

1½ tsp.	pickling salt	7.5 mL
1½ tsp.	sugar	7.5 mL
1½ tsp.	mustard seeds	7.5 mL
	a couple of onion slices	
1	clove garlic	1
½	small hot chili pepper	½
1 tsp.	dill seed	5 mL

Fill up the jars with the asparagus bits to within 1 inch (2.5 cm) of the rim. Pour in the hot pickling liquid, leaving ¼ inch (.6 cm) head space. Wipe the rims clean. Seal according to manufacturer's directions. Process the jars in a boiling water bath for 10 minutes.

Spicy Pickled Green Beans

Makes 4 quart (1-L) jars

Garden favorites, green beans are plentiful and reasonably priced in late summer. Use the longest, straightest beans you can find. Curved or misshapen beans can be pickled too, but the perfect ones are much more impressive.

4 lbs.	green beans	1.8 kg
5 cups	water	1.2 L
5 cups	white vinegar	1.2 L
4 Tbsp.	mustard seeds	60 mL
4 Tbsp.	dill seeds, or 8 – 12 stalks of fresh dill	60 mL
4 Tbsp.	pickling salt	60 mL
8	cloves garlic, peeled	8
8	small hot chili peppers, or 4 tsp. (20 mL) dried chili flakes (optional)	8

Trim the stem ends from the beans and cut to jar length if necessary. When standing upright the beans should be about 1 inch (2.5 cm) below the rim of the jar.

Prepare the preserving jars.

Combine the water and vinegar in your preserving pot and bring to a boil. Reduce the heat to keep the liquid at a simmer.

Working with one jar at a time, place 1 Tbsp. (15 mL) each of mustard seed, dill seed and salt, 2 cloves of garlic, and 2 hot peppers or 1 tsp. (5 mL) dried chili flakes in each jar. Pack the beans tightly into the jar. The easiest way to do this is to lay the jar on its side and place the beans inside by small handfuls. As the jar fills up, stand it upright, and add additional beans one by one. It is important to pack the beans tightly to prevent beans from floating when you add the liquid.

Carefully pour the hot vinegar solution over the beans to within ½ inch (1.2 cm) of the rim. Release the air bubbles. Add additional liquid if necessary, leaving ¼ inch (.6 cm) head space. Wipe the rims clean. Seal according to manufacturer's directions. Repeat with the remaining jars. Process the jars in a boiling water bath for 10 minutes.

Sweet Spiced Pickled Beets

Makes 4 to 5 pint (500-mL) jars

2	3-inch (7.5 cm) cinnamon sticks, broken	2
1 tsp.	each whole cloves and allspice	5 mL
2 cups	red wine vinegar	475 mL
2 cups	water	475 mL
1½ cups	brown sugar	360 mL
1 tsp.	salt	5 mL
4 lbs.	beets, cooked, peeled and sliced if necessary	1.8 kg
2	medium onions, peeled, halved and cut into ¼-inch (.6-cm) slices	2

The pleasant, sweet taste and firm texture of beets makes them a natural for pickling. Small, tender baby beets may be pickled whole, but medium-sized beets up to 2½ inches (6.2 cm) are better sliced. Avoid large beets — they tend to have tough, woody centers.

Prepare the preserving jars. Put the cinnamon sticks, cloves and allspice into a cheesecloth bag and tie the top with string.

Combine the vinegar, water, sugar, salt and the spice bag in your preserving pot. Bring to a boil over medium-high heat and simmer for 5 minutes. Add the beets and onions. Simmer for 5 minutes over medium heat. Discard the spice bag. Leaving the pot on low heat, spoon the beets and onions into hot, sterilized jars. Cover with the hot liquid, leaving ½ inch (1.2 cm) head space. Release the air bubbles. Add additional liquid, leaving ¼ inch (.6 cm) head space. Wipe the rims clean. Seal according to manufacturer's directions. Process the jars in a boiling water bath for 20 minutes.

Note: Never peel beets before cooking or their lovely red color will bleed into the water. Scrub them well, then cut off the tops about 2 inches (5 cm) above the crown. Leave the root end intact. Cook the beets in a saucepan, with just enough water to cover. Simmer 20–30 minutes, until they are barely tender. Drain, cover with ice water and let cool 3–5 minutes. Drain and cut off the tops and root ends. The skins will slip off easily.

Michael's Pickled Onions

Makes 4 to 5 pint (500-mL) jars

4 cups	water	950 mL
1/2 cup	pickling salt	120 mL
3 lbs.	shallots or small white onions, up to 3/4 inch (2 cm) in diameter, peeled (see "How to Peel Onions" page 135)	1.4 kg
2 tsp.	each whole black peppercorns, whole allspice and mustard seeds	10 mL
1 tsp.	dried chili flakes	5 mL
2	1/4-inch (.6-cm) slices of peeled fresh ginger	2
3	bay leaves	3
2 1/2 cups	malt vinegar	600 mL
2 cups	cider vinegar	475 mL
1/4 cup	brown sugar	60 mL

Combine the water and salt in a large bowl. Stir until the salt is dissolved. Add the shallots or onions and mix well. Cover and refrigerate overnight, stirring the mixture 3 or 4 times.

The next day, prepare the preserving jars. Put the pepper-corns, allspice, mustard seeds, chili flakes, ginger and bay leaves into a cheesecloth bag and tie the top with string.

Combine the spice bag, vinegars and sugar in your pre-serving pot. Bring to a boil over medium heat. Simmer gently for 5 minutes; cover and keep hot until you are ready to fill the jars.

Meanwhile, drain the onions in a colander. Cover with cold water and drain again. Do this 3 times; if the onions are not rinsed thoroughly the finished pickle will be too salty. Roll the onions in a clean dish towel to dry them.

Return the pickling liquid to a boil and add the onions. Cook *only* until the liquid returns to a boil. Quickly remove the onions with a slotted spoon and transfer them to the hot, sterilized jars, filling them to within 1 inch (2.5 cm) of the rims. Discard the spice bag. Carefully pour the hot vinegar solution over the onions to within ½ inch (1.2 cm) of the rim. Release the air bubbles. Add additional liquid if necessary. Wipe the rims clean. Seal according to manufacturer's directions. Process the jars in a boiling water bath for 10 minutes.

Pickled Cherries with Tarragon

Makes 4 to 5 pint (500-mL) jars

3 lbs.	firm, ripe, sweet black cherries	1.4 kg
2 cups	red wine vinegar	475 mL
2 cups	water	475 mL
4 tsp.	pickling salt	20 mL
4 tsp.	sugar	20 mL
8	3-inch (7.5-cm) sprigs fresh French tarragon	8

A most unusual condiment. Eat them like olives. This is also delicious made with seedless red grapes.

Prepare the preserving jars.

Trim the stems of the cherries to about 1 inch (2.5 cm). Do not remove the pits. Prick each cherry several times with a needle so the skins don't burst.

Combine the vinegar and water in your preserving pot and bring to a boil over high heat. Reduce the heat to keep the liquid at a simmer.

In each hot, sterilized jar place 1 tsp. (5 mL) each of salt and sugar and 2 sprigs of tarragon. Fill the jars with cherries to 1 inch (2.5 cm) below the rim. Pour the hot liquid into the jars, leaving ½ inch (1.2 cm) head space. Release the air bubbles. Add additional liquid if necessary. Wipe the rims clean. Seal according to manufacturer's directions. Process the jars in a boiling water bath for 10 minutes.

Antipasto Pickles

Makes 7 to 8 pint (500-mL) jars

A wonderful way to pickle a variety of fresh vegetables, this makes an instant appetizer.

4 cups	cauliflower florets, cut into 1 to 1½-inch (2.5- to 3.8-cm) pieces	950 mL
2 cups	unpeeled zucchini, cut into ¼-inch (.6-cm) rounds	475 mL
2 cups	peeled carrots, cut diagonally into ½-inch (1.2-cm) slices	475 mL
2 cups	green beans, cut into 1-inch (2.5-cm) pieces	475 mL
2 cups	celery, cut into sticks 2 inches by ½ inch (5 cm by 1.2 cm)	475 mL
1 cup	red bell pepper, cut into 1-inch (2.5-cm) pieces	240 mL
1 cup	yellow bell pepper, cut into 1-inch (2.5-cm) pieces	240 mL
2 cups	pearl onions, peeled	475 mL
⅔ cup	pickling salt	160 mL
6 cups	cider vinegar	1.5 L
2 cups	water	475 mL
1¼ cups	sugar	300 mL
3 Tbsp.	mustard seeds	45 mL
3 Tbsp.	celery seeds	45 mL
1 Tbsp.	turmeric	15 mL
2 tsp.	coriander seeds	10 mL
2 tsp.	peppercorns	10 mL
7 – 8	bay leaves	7 – 8
7 – 8	cloves garlic, peeled	7 – 8
7 – 8	small red chili peppers	7 – 8

Combine all the vegetables in a large bowl.

Bring 6 cups (1.5 L) of water to a boil. Add the salt and stir until dissolved. Let cool. Pour the cooled brine over the vegetables. It should cover them completely; add more water if necessary. Place a weighted plate on top of the vegetables to keep them submerged. Cover and let stand overnight.

The next day, drain the vegetables in a colander. Rinse thoroughly in cold water, then drain again. Set aside.

Prepare the preserving jars.

Combine the vinegar, water, sugar, mustard seeds, celery seeds, turmeric, coriander seeds and peppercorns in your preserving pot. Bring to a boil over medium-high heat and boil for 5 minutes. Add the vegetables and return to a boil. Reduce the heat to medium and simmer for another 5 minutes, stirring constantly to mix the vegetables thoroughly.

In each hot, sterilized jar place 1 bay leaf, 1 clove of garlic and 1 chili pepper. Using a slotted spoon, remove the vegetables from the pot, and divide them among the jars. Quickly bring the hot liquid in the pot to a boil and pour over the vegetables, distributing the spices evenly and leaving ¼ inch (.6 cm) head space. (If you don't have enough liquid, top up with additional vinegar.) Release the air bubbles. Wipe the rims clean. Seal according to manufacturer's directions. Process the jars in a boiling water bath for 10 minutes.

How to Peel Onions (or Shallots)

Place the onions in a large bowl and add enough boiling water to cover them. Let stand 2 – 3 minutes. Pour off the hot water. Place the bowl in the sink and run cold water into the bowl to cool the onions quickly. Drain in a colander. Using a sharp knife, remove only the minimum at the base and tip of the onions and peel away the outer skin.

A very elegant pickle.
Serve it as an accom-
paniment to roasted
meats. Be sure that
the pears are firm and
not overly ripe.

Pickled Pears with Honey and Red Wine

Makes about 6 pint (500-mL) jars

1½ cups	honey	360 mL
2½ cups	red wine vinegar	600 mL
2½ cups	full-bodied red wine	600 mL
6	3-inch (7.5-cm) cinnamon sticks	6
1	lemon, zest only, cut in a continuous spiral	1
5 lbs.	small firm-ripe pears	2.25 kg
	whole cloves	

In your preserving pot, combine the honey, vinegar, red wine, cinnamon sticks and lemon zest. Bring to a boil over medium heat and simmer 10 minutes, stirring occasionally.

Peel, core and halve the pears. Stick 2 cloves into each half. Add the pears to the simmering liquid and poach them gently for about 10 minutes. They should be just barely tender. Turn them frequently. Remove from the heat, cool slightly and cover with a clean dish towel. Leave the pears to stand overnight in the syrup.

The next day, prepare the preserving jars. Using a slotted spoon, remove the pears and cinnamon sticks from the syrup and set aside. Discard the lemon zest.

Bring the syrup quickly to a boil over high heat, and boil rapidly for 10 minutes. Place the pears cut side down in the hot, sterilized jars, overlapping them slightly. Place 1 cinnamon stick in each jar. Pour the boiling syrup over the pears, leaving ½ inch (1.2 cm) head space. Release the air bubbles. Add additional syrup if necessary. Wipe the rims clean. Seal according to manufacturer's directions. Process the jars in a boiling water bath for 10 minutes.

Relishes

The word relish summons up vivid pictures of outdoor summer fun—impromptu barbecues or picnics on the beach. But relishes are much more than just simple sauces for hamburgers and hot dogs. These zesty condiments can add a special zing to grilled lamb chops, a roast pork loin or even fish. You can serve relishes with smoked meats, cheeses or any bland dish that needs a little perking up.

Tangy, spicy medleys of vegetables or sometimes fruit, relishes are basically just a chopped pickle. The ingredients for relish may be sliced, coarsely chopped, shredded or ground, but are all of a uniform size. A food processor makes short work of preparing vegetables for relish. Vegetables with a high water content, such as zucchini, cucumbers and onions, are usually salted beforehand to draw out moisture, which reduces the amount of cooking time required. Salting also helps larger pieces of vegetables to retain their shape and texture.

Relishes are cooked quickly—the vegetables are simmered in a vinegar-based syrup just long enough to ensure that they are heated throughout. Vegetables should be barely tender, retaining some of their original crisp character.

This brief cooking time is one way that relishes are distinguished from chutneys. In chutney-making, a long, slow simmering reduces the ingredients to a soft pulp.

Properly made relish will be moist but not watery. In some recipes, a little cornstarch or flour is added at the end of the cooking period to thicken the relish and lightly bind the ingredients together. Relishes also tend to thicken up slightly in the jar, as the vegetables absorb some of the vinegar syrup.

Relishes can be mild or fiery, sweet or tangy, peppery or pungent. Hot peppers, spices and seasonings can be added or subtracted to suit your own personal tastes.

Savory relishes sharpen the tastebuds and surprise the palate. They can heighten our enjoyment of everyday foods or contribute a unique finishing touch to any meal.

Carrot and Cucumber Relish

Makes about 5 to 6 8-oz. (250-mL) jars

A simple, old-fashioned relish perfect with cold sliced meats or barbecued burgers.

4 cups	finely chopped, unpeeled cucumbers (about 5–6 medium)	950 mL
2 cups	grated carrots (about 6–7 medium)	475 mL
1 cup	finely chopped onion	240 mL
3 Tbsp.	pickling salt	45 mL
1½ cups	cider vinegar	360 mL
1½ cups	sugar	360 mL
2 tsp.	mustard seeds	10 mL
2 tsp.	celery seeds	10 mL
1 tsp.	fennel seeds	5 mL

In a large bowl, combine the cucumbers, carrots, onion and salt. Mix well and let stand 3–4 hours.

The next day, drain the vegetables in a colander. Rinse them and press out as much water as possible. Set aside.

Prepare the preserving jars.

Combine the remaining ingredients in your preserving pot. Bring to a boil over medium-high heat. Reduce the heat and simmer for 10 minutes. Add the drained vegetables. Increase the heat again and once the mixture has returned to a boil, cook, stirring often, for about 10 minutes, until most of the liquid has been absorbed. Don't worry if the relish seems to be too liquid; it will thicken up a little as it cools.

Remove from the heat. Spoon the relish into hot, sterilized jars, leaving ½ inch (1.2 cm) head space. Release the air bubbles. Wipe the rims clean. Seal according to manufacturer's directions. Process the jars in a boiling water bath for 10 minutes.

Previous page, from left to right: *Ripe Tomato Relish (p.144), Old-Time Corn Relish (p. 142), and Pepper Relish (p. 147).*

Facing page: *Feisty Red Pepper Ketchup (p. 176).*

Many different versions of chow chow can be found in old-time cookbooks. This is a relish type—made with ground vegetables. There is also a chunky vegetable chow chow, which is more like a mixed pickle. You can chop the vegetables by hand or use a food processor if you prefer.

Chow Chow

Makes about 6 pint (500-mL) jars

7 lbs.	green tomatoes, chopped very finely	3.2 kg
5	medium green or red bell peppers, cored, seeded and chopped very finely	5
5	medium onions, peeled and chopped very finely	5
¼ cup	pickling salt	60 mL
2½ cups	cider vinegar	600 mL
1½ cups	sugar	360 mL
¼ cup	mixed pickling spice tied in a cheesecloth bag	60 mL
2 tsp.	dry English mustard	10 mL

Combine the vegetables and salt in a large bowl. Mix well. Cover and let stand overnight.

The next day, drain the vegetables in a colander, pressing out excess moisture. Set aside.

Prepare the preserving jars. Combine the remaining ingredients in your preserving pot. Bring to a boil over medium-high heat. Simmer for 10 minutes. Add the drained vegetables. Once the mixture returns to a boil, reduce the heat to medium and simmer for 15 minutes, stirring often.

Remove from the heat; discard the spice bag. Spoon the relish into hot, sterilized jars, leaving ½ inch (1.2 cm) head space. Release the air bubbles. Wipe the rims clean. Seal according to manufacturer's directions. Process the jars in a boiling water bath for 15 minutes.

Quick Dip

Mix homemade relish with sour cream or plain yogurt for an instant dip for fresh vegetables.

Nectarine and Pepper Relish

Makes about 6 to 7 8-oz. (250-mL) jars

6 cups	coarsely chopped firm-ripe nectarines	1.5 L
2 cups	coarsely chopped red bell peppers	475 mL
1 cup	finely chopped onions	240 mL
¼ cup	pickling salt	60 mL
1½ cups	brown sugar	360 mL
¾ cup	cider vinegar	180 mL
1 cup	dark raisins	240 mL
2 tsp.	mustard seeds	10 mL
1 tsp.	cinnamon	5 mL
1 tsp.	nutmeg	5 mL
½ tsp.	cloves	2.5 mL
½ tsp.	ginger	2.5 mL

A sweet and spicy relish that is delectable with roast pork, chicken or baked ham. You can substitute peaches or pears for the nectarines, but be sure to use fruit that is quite firm or it will turn to mush during cooking.

Combine the nectarines, peppers, onions and salt in a large bowl. Let stand at room temperature for 3 hours. Drain well in a colander, rinse thoroughly and drain again, pressing to remove as much liquid as possible.

Prepare the preserving jars.

In your preserving pot, combine the remaining ingredients and bring to a boil over medium-high heat. Stir in the fruit and vegetable mixture. Simmer, stirring often, for about 30 minutes, or until the mixture starts to thicken.

Remove from the heat. Spoon the relish into hot, sterilized jars, leaving ½ inch (1.2 cm) head space. Release the air bubbles. Wipe the rims clean. Seal according to manufacturer's directions. Process the jars in a boiling water bath for 15 minutes.

Old-Time Corn Relish

Makes about 4 to 5 pint (500-mL) jars

Make this classic country relish in September when corn is at its best and sweetest. You can also use drained, canned corn kernels or frozen corn that has been defrosted and drained.

To make a curried corn relish, add 2 tsp. (10 mL) curry powder and 1 tsp. (5 mL) liquid hot pepper seasoning along with the other spices.

5 cups	fresh corn kernels (about 10 ears)	1.2 L
1 cup	finely chopped red bell peppers	240 mL
1/2 cup	finely chopped green bell peppers	120 mL
1 cup	finely chopped onion	240 mL
1/2 cup	finely chopped celery	120 mL
1 3/4 cups	cider vinegar	420 mL
3/4 cup	sugar	180 mL
1 1/2 tsp.	salt	7.5 mL
2 tsp.	celery seed	10 mL
1 1/2 tsp.	dry English mustard	7.5 mL
1/2 tsp.	turmeric	2.5 mL
2 Tbsp.	flour (optional)	30 mL

Prepare the preserving jars.

If you are using fresh corn, husk it and cook the ears for 10 minutes in a pot of boiling water. Drain, then plunge the corn into ice water to cool quickly so it can be handled easily. Standing the ears of corn on end, cut the kernels carefully off the cobs using a very sharp knife. Do not scrape the cobs — the milky juice will make the relish cloudy.

Combine the red and green peppers, onion, celery, vinegar, sugar, salt, celery seed, mustard and turmeric in your preserving pot. Bring to a boil over medium heat and simmer for 10 minutes, stirring occasionally. Add the corn and simmer another 5 minutes, stirring often.

If you desire a slightly thicker relish, combine the flour with 1/4 cup (60 mL) cold water in a small measuring cup. Mix until smooth, then add to the relish when you add the corn. Take care to stir the relish often, as the thickened relish may tend to stick to the bottom of the pot.

Remove from the heat. Spoon the relish into hot, sterilized jars, leaving ½ inch (1.2 cm) head space. Release the air bubbles. Wipe the rims clean. Seal according to manufacturer's directions. Process the jars in a boiling water bath for 15 minutes.

Beet and Red Cabbage Relish

Makes about 4 to 5 pint (500-mL) jars

15	beets, about 2 inches (5 cm) across, cooked, peeled and shredded (about 4 lbs./1.8 kg)	15
½	medium red cabbage, shredded	½
1½ cups	finely chopped celery	360 mL
1½ cups	finely chopped onion	360 mL
1 cup	cranberry or orange juice	240 mL
1½ cups	red wine vinegar	360 mL
1½ cups	brown sugar	360 mL
2 Tbsp.	prepared creamed horseradish	30 mL
1 Tbsp.	finely grated orange zest	15 mL
1½ tsp.	salt	7.5 mL
½ tsp.	cloves	2.5 mL
½ tsp.	allspice	2.5 mL

For a truly unusual sandwich, blend softened cream cheese with a little horseradish and spread on hearty, preferably homemade bread. Top with sliced, rare roast beef and a dollop of this relish.

Prepare the preserving jars.

Combine all the ingredients in your preserving pot and bring to a boil over medium heat, stirring occasionally. Simmer 20–25 minutes, stirring often.

Remove from the heat. Spoon the relish into hot, sterilized jars, leaving ½ inch (1.2 cm) head space. Release the air bubbles. Wipe the rims clean. Seal according to manufacturer's directions. Process the jars in a boiling water bath for 10 minutes.

Ripe Tomato Relish

Makes about 4 to 5 pint (500-mL) jars

Take advantage of a bountiful tomato crop and cook up a batch of this hearty relish. Serve it alongside homemade macaroni and cheese or meat loaf.

12 cups	chopped tomatoes, preferably plum or Roma	3 L
2 cups	chopped onions	475 mL
1 cup	chopped red bell pepper	240 mL
1 cup	chopped celery	240 mL
3 Tbsp.	pickling salt	45 mL
1 cup	red wine vinegar	240 mL
2 cups	brown sugar	475 mL
3 Tbsp.	mustard seeds	45 mL
1 Tbsp.	dried chili flakes	15 mL
1 tsp.	each cloves, cinnamon and nutmeg	5 mL

Prepare the preserving jars. Combine the tomatoes, onion, pepper and celery in a large bowl. Sprinkle with the salt and stir well. Let stand for 15 minutes. Drain well in a colander, pressing to remove as much liquid as possible. Do not rinse.

Combine the remaining ingredients in your preserving pot and bring to a boil over medium heat. Add the drained vegetables. Simmer, stirring often, for 30–50 minutes, or until the relish is slightly thickened. If the tomatoes are especially juicy, the cooking time will be longer.

Remove from the heat. Ladle the relish into hot, sterilized jars, leaving ½ inch (1.2 cm) head space. Release the air bubbles. Wipe the rims clean. Seal according to manufacturer's directions. Process the jars in a boiling water bath for 15 minutes.

Spicy Ripe Tomato Relish. Add 3 jalapeño peppers, seeded and finely chopped, to the vegetables during the salting stage, and ¼ cup (60 mL) prepared creamed horseradish when the vegetables are added to the boiling liquid.

Salsa Fiesta!

Makes about 5 to 6 pint (500-mL) jars

8 cups	coarsely chopped tomatoes	2 L
2 cups	coarsely chopped onions	475 mL
1 cup	coarsely chopped green bell peppers	240 mL
1 cup	finely chopped, seeded jalapeño peppers (see "Handling Hot Peppers," page 118)	240 mL
6	large cloves garlic, finely chopped	6
1/4 cup	finely chopped fresh coriander	60 mL
2/3 cup	red wine vinegar or lemon juice	160 mL
1 Tbsp.	salt	15 mL
1 tsp.	white pepper	5 mL

How hot is this salsa? It all depends on your tolerance for spicy foods. I consider it medium-hot. If hot peppers make you nervous, cut the amount of jalapeño peppers in half, or leave them out altogether, substituting extra green peppers instead.

Prepare the preserving jars.

Combine all the ingredients in your preserving pot and bring to a boil over medium-high heat. Reduce the heat to medium and simmer, stirring often, for 20 minutes.

Remove from the heat. Ladle the salsa into hot, sterilized jars, leaving 1/2 inch (1.2 cm) head space. Wipe the rims clean. Seal according to manufacturer's directions. Process the jars in a boiling water bath for 20 minutes.

Chunky Salsa Guacamole

Instead of serving salsa and guacamole separately, use this colorful dip as an all-in-one topping for tacos or a zesty accompaniment for chicken or fish.

Simply toss 1 cup (240 mL) of salsa with 1 peeled, diced avocado. Sprinkle with a little lemon juice, season with salt and freshly ground pepper and garnish with 1 Tbsp. (15 mL) finely chopped fresh coriander.

India Relish

Makes about 5 to 6 pint (500-mL) jars

This classic mixed vegetable relish was traditionally made in the autumn to use up garden surpluses. The quickest and easiest way to prepare the vegetables is to shred them in a food processor. India Relish is an excellent accompaniment to lamb or pork.

4 cups	chopped green cabbage	950 mL
1 cup	chopped green bell pepper	240 mL
1 cup	chopped red bell pepper	240 mL
2 cups	chopped onions	475 mL
6 cups	grated zucchini	1.5 L
2 cups	grated carrots	475 mL
1/4 cup	pickling salt	60 mL
11/2 cups	brown sugar	360 mL
3 cups	cider vinegar	720 mL
1 tsp.	each ginger, coriander and curry powder	5 mL
1/2 tsp.	each turmeric and cumin	2.5 mL
4 tsp.	dry English mustard	20 mL

In a large bowl, combine the cabbage, green and red peppers, onion, zucchini, carrots and salt. Cover and let stand 3–4 hours. Drain the vegetables in a colander, pressing out excess liquid. Return the drained vegetables to the bowl.

Combine the remaining ingredients in your preserving pot. Bring to a boil over high heat and boil rapidly for 5 minutes. Pour the mixture over the vegetables in the bowl, and stir to combine. Let stand, uncovered, at room temperature until cool, about 2 hours.

Prepare the preserving jars.

Drain the liquid from the vegetables into your preserving pot. Bring to a full boil over high heat and stir in the vegetables. Once the mixture returns to a boil, reduce the heat to medium and simmer for 10–15 minutes, until the vegetables are thoroughly hot, stirring constantly.

Remove from the heat. Spoon the relish into hot, sterilized jars, leaving ½ inch (1.2 cm) head space. Release the air bubbles. Wipe the rims clean. Seal according to manufacturer's directions. Process the jars in a boiling water bath for 15 minutes.

Pepper Relish

Makes about 5 to 6 8-oz. (250-mL) jars

3 cups	finely chopped red bell peppers	720 mL
3 cups	finely chopped green bell peppers	720 mL
2 cups	finely chopped onion	475 mL
2 cups	cider vinegar	475 mL
1 cup	sugar	240 mL
2 Tbsp.	mixed pickling spice tied in a cheesecloth bag	30 mL
2 tsp.	crushed red chili flakes	10 mL
2 tsp.	salt	10 mL

Use any combination of red, green, yellow or orange peppers for this relish, or substitute some hot peppers if you like. Just be sure that the total amount matches the recipe. Don't use all green peppers or you'll end up with relish that is an unattractive muddy color.

Prepare the preserving jars.

Combine the peppers and onions in a large bowl. Add enough boiling water to cover them. Let stand 5 minutes. Drain thoroughly in a colander, pressing to remove excess moisture.

Combine the remaining ingredients in your preserving pot and bring to a boil over high heat. Add the drained vegetables. Reduce the heat to medium and simmer, stirring occasionally, for 25–30 minutes.

Remove from the heat; discard the spice bag. Spoon the relish into hot, sterilized jars, leaving ½ inch (1.2 cm) head space. Release the air bubbles. Wipe the rims clean. Seal according to manufacturer's directions. Process the jars in a boiling water bath for 10 minutes.

Zesty Zucchini Relish

Makes about 5 to 6 8-oz. (250-mL) jars

Nothing like it with burgers, European weiners or grilled Italian sausages on crusty French rolls. You can use a food processor to shred the vegetables.

6 cups	grated zucchini, unpeeled	1.5 L
1 cup	grated carrot	240 mL
2 cups	finely chopped onion	475 mL
1 cup	finely chopped red bell pepper	240 mL
1 cup	finely chopped green bell pepper	240 mL
2 – 3	jalapeño peppers, seeded and finely chopped	2 – 3
1/4 cup	pickling salt	60 mL
2 cups	sugar	475 mL
2 cups	herb vinegar, divided	475 mL
2 tsp.	celery seed	10 mL
1 tsp.	red chili flakes	5 mL
1/2 tsp.	each cinnamon, nutmeg, turmeric and freshly ground black pepper	2.5 mL
2 tsp.	cornstarch	10 mL
1½ tsp.	dry English mustard	7.5 mL

Combine the vegetables and pickling salt in a large bowl. Mix well. Cover with ice and refrigerate overnight.

The next day, prepare the preserving jars. Drain the vegetables in a colander; rinse well and squeeze out excess moisture. (An efficient way to do this is to line the colander with cheesecloth before rinsing the vegetables under running water; then you can gather up the corners of the cloth and squeeze out the moisture.)

Combine the sugar, 1½ cups (360 mL) of the vinegar, and the celery seed, chili flakes and ground spices in your preserving pot. Bring to a boil over high heat, stirring until the sugar is dissolved. Stir in the drained vegetables. Reduce the heat to medium and simmer about 30 minutes, stirring often, until the mixture begins to thicken and a lot of the liquid has been absorbed.

In a measuring cup or small bowl, stir the cornstarch and mustard together with a fork. Gradually pour in the remaining ½ cup (120 mL) vinegar, stirring to form a smooth paste. Stir into the relish. Cook another 5 minutes, stirring constantly, until the liquid clears and thickens.

Remove from the heat. Spoon the relish into hot, sterilized jars, leaving ½ inch (1.2 cm) head space. Release the air bubbles. Wipe the rims clean. Seal according to manufacturer's directions. Process the jars in a boiling water bath for 10 minutes.

About Chilies

Chilies originated in Latin America, and are members of the capsicum family. There are a vast variety of chili types — more than 100 varieties in Mexico alone. Chilies differ in size, shape, color and strength; the most commonly available to North Americans are small, thin, green or red chilies from 1 to 4 inches (2.5 to 10 cm) long. As a very general rule of thumb, the smaller, thinner and darker the chili, the more fiery it will be. Fresh green chilies are usually milder than dried ones. Many types of seasonings are made from chilies; among them are chili powder, cayenne pepper, paprika, dried chili flakes and prepared chili sauces. Chilies may be used whole, either fresh or dried, to spice up many types of pickles or chopped fresh into relishes or chutneys. Dried chili flakes are an excellent substitute for fresh chilies.

Cranberry, Pear and Apple Relish

Makes about 6 to 7 8-oz. (250-mL) jars

Use Granny Smith or any type of crisp, tart apple that will not disintegrate during cooking. This is a fresh, exciting alternative to traditional cranberry sauce.

1 cup	cranberry or apple juice	240 mL
1½ cups	sugar	360 mL
¾ cup	cider vinegar	180 mL
½ tsp.	salt	2.5 mL
½ tsp.	cloves	2.5 mL
½ tsp.	allspice	2.5 mL
1	3-inch (7.5-cm) cinnamon stick	1
3 cups	cranberries	720 mL
3	firm-ripe pears, peeled, cored and chopped	3
3	Granny Smith apples, peeled, cored and chopped	3
½ cup	finely chopped red onion	120 mL

Prepare the preserving jars.

In your preserving pot, combine the cranberry or apple juice, sugar, vinegar, salt, cloves, allspice and cinnamon stick. Bring to a boil over medium-high heat. Stir in the remaining ingredients. Reduce the heat to medium and simmer, stirring often, for 20–25 minutes, until the mixture begins to thicken.

Remove from the heat. Discard the cinnamon stick. Spoon the relish into hot, sterilized jars, leaving ½ inch (1.2 cm) head space. Release the air bubbles. Wipe the rims clean. Seal according to manufacturer's directions. Process the jars in a boiling water bath for 10 minutes.

Zesty Cranberry Relish. Omit the cloves, allspice and cinnamon and add ¼ cup (60 mL) creamed prepared horseradish.

Chutneys

A distinctive, pungent condiment of Indian origin, chutney has a characteristic sweet and sour flavor and a soft jam-like texture; it is usually much smoother and slightly sweeter than traditional pickle relishes.

In India, chutneys are commonly made fresh before each meal, with a considerable amount of toasting, grinding and blending of whole spices.

Western-style chutneys, whether store-bought or home-made, are quite different from their authentic Indian counterparts. Fruits or vegetables, sugar, vinegar and spices are gently simmered to form a thick, soft pulp, somewhat like a chunky ketchup. A rich, mellow flavor is achieved by long, slow cooking and additional complexity develops as chutney matures in the jar.

Chutney can be made from virtually any mixture of fruits, and an endless variety of spices can be used to enhance the taste. Exotic and intriguing, chutneys exhibit great diversity in flavor — from mild and sweet to fiery and piquant. You can turn up the heat by adding one or two finely chopped chili peppers or reduce it by omitting or cutting back on peppers and hot spices.

Be enthusiastic with spices. Chutney is supposed to be aromatic, exotic and flavorful — a bland, boring chutney is a waste of time. Once you have gained some confidence, experiment with new combinations of fruit, vegetables and spices. Tried and true recipes will always be classics, but part of the fun and creativity of making chutney is going beyond the recipe and trying something new. Just keep in mind the ratios of fruit, vinegar and sugar.

Making chutney affords an excellent opportunity to use up less than perfect produce. Provided that the bruised or damaged portions are removed, you can safely use slightly blemished or misshapen fruit.

Another advantage of chutney is that it is not necessarily a seasonal preserve, but may be made from fresh or dried fruit and vegetables that are available throughout the year. Combinations can vary depending on personal taste and ingredients at hand.

A crucial stage of chutney-making is the storage and maturation of the finished product. Don't be tempted to taste your chutney too soon, but give the flavors a chance to mingle and mellow. Like a fine wine, your chutney will develop as it ages; you'll be amazed at how much the flavor intensifies with time.

Traditionally served with curried dishes, chutney has a myriad uses — in appetizers, salads, main courses, even desserts. It is superb with any kind of hot or cold roasted meat or poultry and great for a nibble with cheese and crackers, especially robust cheeses like Stilton or Gorgonzola. Chutney brings sparkle to everyday foods such as burgers, meat loaf or chops. Add a dollop to a stir-fry, or spread a little on a sandwich in place of mayonnaise. Illuminate vegetarian meals by spooning chutney over baked potatoes, squash or steamed vegetables, or add it to an omelette. Enjoy a delicious snack of a toasted bagel spread with cream cheese and topped with chutney. Mix it into your homemade stuffing for roast turkey or chicken.

Creative cooks can incorporate chutney as an ingredient in dips, salad dressings and sauces. It can even be made into sorbet.

Chutney is terrific!

Jar Size

The recipes in this chapter denote 8-oz. (250-mL) jars, but feel free to use pint (500-mL) jars if you use chutney frequently.

Mango Chutney

Makes about 7 to 8 8-oz. (250-mL) jars

Mango chutney is what most often comes to mind when chutney is mentioned. Mangoes seem to be most reasonably priced in May. This recipe works equally well with peaches or papayas. Mango chutney is a traditional accompaniment for curried dishes.

5	large mangoes, barely ripe	5
1½ cups	cider vinegar	360 mL
1 cup	demerara sugar	240 mL
½ cup	finely chopped onion	120 mL
½ cup	finely chopped red bell pepper	120 mL
½ cup	finely chopped green bell pepper	120 mL
¼ cup	fresh ginger, minced	60 mL
½ cup	lime juice	120 mL
2 tsp.	salt	10 mL
1 Tbsp.	mustard seeds	15 mL
1 Tbsp.	dried chili flakes	15 mL
½ cup	chopped dried apricots	120 mL

Prepare the preserving jars. Peel the mangoes and slice the pulp away from the pit. Cut into chunks.

Combine all the ingredients in your preserving pot and bring to a boil over medium heat. Simmer, stirring often, for 45–60 minutes, until the mixture starts to thicken. Reduce the heat to low. If there is a lot of liquid on the surface of the chutney, skim off as much as possible and place it in a small saucepan. Boil hard until the liquid is reduced by half, then stir it back into the chutney. Bring the chutney back to a boil.

Remove from the heat. Ladle into hot, sterilized jars, leaving ½ inch (1.2 cm) head space. Wipe the rims clean. Seal according to manufacturer's directions. Process the jars in a boiling water bath for 10 minutes.

Banango Chutney. Replace the 5 mangoes with 3 mangoes and 4 bananas, sliced.

Plum Chutney with Cinnamon and Coriander

Makes about 6 to 7 8-oz. (250-mL) jars

A dark and delicious chutney with an assertive flavor, this is especially good with barbecued pork, lamb or chicken.

6 cups	chopped purple or red plums	1.5 L
1 cup	finely chopped apple	240 mL
1 cup	finely chopped onion	240 mL
2 cups	brown sugar	475 mL
1½ cups	red wine vinegar	360 mL
½ cup	chopped prunes	120 mL
1 Tbsp.	mustard seeds	15 mL
2 tsp.	dried chili flakes	10 mL
2 tsp.	salt	10 mL
2 tsp.	cinnamon	10 mL
2 tsp.	coriander seeds	10 mL

Prepare the preserving jars.

Combine all the ingredients in your preserving pot. Bring to a boil over medium-high heat, stirring occasionally. Reduce the heat to medium and simmer, stirring often, for 45–60 minutes, until the chutney is thick enough to mound on a spoon.

Remove from the heat. Ladle the chutney into hot, sterilized jars, leaving ½ inch (1.2 cm) head space. Wipe the rims clean. Seal according to manufacturer's directions. Process the jars in a boiling water bath for 10 minutes.

Previous page: *Mango Chutney (p. 154)*.

Facing page, foreground: *Salsa Fiesta! (p.145)*; background: *Fresh Fruit Salsa (p.199)*.

Pineapple and Papaya Chutney

Makes about 4 to 5 8-oz. (250-mL) jars

A sweet, succulent chutney redolent of the flavors of the tropics. For a new twist on chicken salad, mix a spoonful or two of this chutney in with the mayonnaise.

3 cups	pineapple, cut into ½-inch (1.2-cm) dice	720 mL
2 cups	papaya, cut into ½-inch (1.2-cm) dice	475 mL
1 cup	finely chopped onion	240 mL
2	small chili peppers, seeded and minced	2
2 cups	brown sugar	475 mL
1½ cups	cider vinegar	360 mL
½ cup	chopped dates	120 mL
2 Tbsp.	grated fresh ginger	30 mL
1	lime, juice and finely grated zest	1
1 tsp.	cinnamon	5 mL
½ tsp.	salt	2.5 mL
½ tsp.	allspice	2.5 mL

Prepare the preserving jars. Combine all the ingredients in your preserving pot. Bring to a boil over medium-high heat. Reduce the heat to medium and simmer, stirring often, for 45–60 minutes, or until the chutney is thick enough to mound on a spoon.

Remove from the heat. Spoon the chutney into hot, sterilized jars, leaving ½ inch (1.2 cm) head space. Wipe the rims clean. Seal according to manufacturer's directions. Process the jars in a boiling water bath for 10 minutes.

About Coriander

A member of the parsley family, coriander has a sweet, orangey aroma and a fresh flavor that is somewhat mild compared to other spices. Coriander is available powdered or as seeds; the seeds are an ingredient in pickling spice and in many spice mixtures used in Indian cooking. Coriander leaves are popular in Asian and Mexican cooking.

Blueberry Chutney

Makes about 4 to 5 8-oz. (250-mL) jars

5 cups	blueberries	1.2 L
1	medium-sized tart apple, peeled, cored and grated	1
1 cup	finely chopped onion	240 mL
1½ cups	red wine vinegar	360 mL
1 cup	brown sugar	240 mL
⅔ cup	maple syrup	160 mL
½ cup	dark raisins	120 mL
1 Tbsp.	finely grated lemon zest	15 mL
2 tsp.	mustard seeds	10 mL
½ tsp.	salt	2.5 mL
½ tsp.	ginger	2.5 mL
½ tsp.	cinnamon	2.5 mL
¼ tsp.	cloves	1.2 mL
¼ tsp.	nutmeg	1.2 mL
¼ tsp.	cayenne pepper	1.2 mL

Surprise the palate with the intriguing combination of flavors in this scrumptious chutney. Blend it half and half with plain yogurt and spoon it over a fresh fruit salad, or try it with grilled salmon.

Prepare the preserving jars.

Place the blueberries in your preserving pot and crush them with a potato masher. Add the remaining ingredients. Bring to a boil over medium-high heat. Reduce the heat to medium and simmer, stirring often, for 45–60 minutes, or until the chutney is thick enough to mound on a spoon.

Remove from the heat. Ladle the chutney into hot, sterilized jars, leaving ½ inch (1.2 cm) head space. Wipe the rims clean. Seal according to manufacturer's directions. Process the jars in a boiling water bath for 10 minutes.

Fig and Lemon Chutney

Makes about 4 to 5 8-oz. (250-mL) jars

A memorable chutney with an exotic twist. The tart flavor goes particularly well with game.

3 – 4	medium lemons	3 – 4
1 tsp.	whole allspice	5 mL
1 tsp.	whole cloves	5 mL
1	3-inch (7.5-cm) stick cinnamon, broken	1
1 lb.	dried figs, cut into ½-inch (1.2-cm) pieces	454 g
½ cup	finely chopped onion	120 mL
1½ cups	cider vinegar	360 mL
¾ cup	sugar	180 mL
½ cup	honey	120 mL
¼ cup	chopped candied ginger	60 mL
1 tsp.	salt	5 mL

Slice the lemons in half lengthwise. Place the cut side down and slice the lemons very thinly, discarding the ends and seeds. You will need 2 cups (475 mL) of sliced lemon. Place the lemon slices in a small bowl and add enough water to cover them. Cover the bowl and let stand overnight at room temperature.

The next day, prepare the preserving jars.

Put the allspice, cloves and cinnamon stick in a cheesecloth bag and tie the top with string.

Drain the lemons in a colander. Combine the lemons and the remaining ingredients in your preserving pot and bring to a boil over medium-high heat. Reduce the heat to medium and simmer, stirring often, for 1 – 1½ hours, or until the chutney is thick enough to mound on a spoon. You may need to add a little water if the mixture gets too thick before the figs are plump.

Remove from the heat. Discard the spice bag. Spoon the chutney into hot, sterilized jars, leaving ½ inch (1.2 cm) head space. Wipe the rims clean. Seal according to manufacturer's directions. Process the jars in a boiling water bath for 10 minutes.

Cranberry, Orange and Apricot Chutney

Makes about 4 to 5 8-oz. (250-mL) jars

1	orange	1
4 cups	cranberries	950 mL
½ cup	finely chopped onion	120 mL
1 cup	chopped dried apricots	240 mL
¾ cup	cider vinegar	180 mL
¾ cup	orange juice	180 mL
½ cup	water	120 mL
2 cups	brown sugar	475 mL
½ tsp.	each cloves, ginger and allspice	2.5 mL

Dress up curry, poultry or ham with this flavorful chutney. It's also delicious with cold meats — try some on a chicken or turkey sandwich.

Prepare the preserving jars.

Slice the orange very thinly, discarding the ends and seeds. Chop very finely.

Combine all the ingredients in your preserving pot and bring to a boil over medium heat. Simmer, stirring often, for about 20 minutes, or until the mixture thickens.

Remove from the heat. Ladle into hot, sterilized jars, leaving ½ inch (1.2 cm) head space. Wipe the rims clean. Seal according to manufacturer's directions. Process the jars in a boiling water bath for 10 minutes.

Carrot and Coconut Chutney

Makes about 8 to 9 8-oz. (250-mL) jars

The slightly larger yield of this recipe will give you some extra jars for gift-giving. This piquant and colorful chutney can be made at any time of the year. You can make an interesting spread for celery or crackers by blending 1/2 cup (120 mL) chutney with 1 cup (240 mL) cream cheese.

4 lbs.	carrots (about 24 medium)	1.8 kg
2	oranges	2
1	lemon	1
2 1/2 cups	brown sugar	600 mL
1 1/2 cups	cider vinegar	360 mL
1 cup	flaked coconut	240 mL
1/2 cup	chopped dried apricots	120 mL
2 Tbsp.	grated fresh ginger	30 mL
1 Tbsp.	mustard seeds	15 mL
1 Tbsp.	dried chili flakes	15 mL
1 tsp.	salt	5 mL
1	3-inch (7.5-cm) cinnamon stick, broken	1

Peel and slice the carrots. Cook them in boiling water until soft, about 35–40 minutes. Drain, then mash or purée the carrots until they are quite smooth. Measure the mashed carrots; you should have about 5 cups (1.2 L).

Using a sharp knife, peel the zest from the oranges and lemon, including as little of the white pith as possible. Cut the peel into very thin shreds. Set aside. Trim away any excess pith from the oranges and lemon. Slice the fruit, then chop it finely, discarding the seeds.

Combine the sugar, vinegar and orange and lemon zest in your preserving pot. Bring the mixture to a boil over medium heat. Reduce the heat to low, cover and simmer for 5 minutes.

Prepare the preserving jars.

Add the carrots, chopped oranges and lemon and the remaining ingredients to the preserving pot. Increase the heat to medium and simmer for 30 – 40 minutes, stirring often, until the chutney has thickened. Stir the chutney almost constantly during the last 10 – 15 minutes of cooking to prevent scorching.

Remove from the heat. Ladle the chutney into hot, sterilized jars, leaving ½ inch (1.2 cm) head space. Wipe the rims clean. Seal according to manufacturer's directions. Process the jars in a boiling water bath for 10 minutes.

About Fresh Ginger

What we often refer to as ginger *root* is actually not a root at all, but a rhizome — a tuber-like stem. When purchasing fresh ginger, look for firm, fresh "hands" with smooth, unblemished skin. Try to select ginger that has as few knobs as possible — it will be easier to peel. Avoid shriveled or moldy-looking ginger that is definitely past its prime.

If you will be using the ginger right away, just store it unwrapped in the crisper drawer of your refrigerator. For longer storage — up to about 3 weeks — wrap it first in a paper towel and then in a plastic bag. Old ginger dries out and loses its flavor.

To peel ginger, remove the tough outer skin by peeling it away with a sharp paring knife or a vegetable peeler, exposing the flesh. Most recipes call for finely chopped or grated fresh ginger, which are essentially the same thing. The quickest way to chop ginger is using a food processor fitted with the steel blade. Simply drop the ginger in through the feed tube while the motor is running. To chop ginger using a French knife, slice the peeled ginger very thinly, then mince. To grate, use the finest surface of a stainless steel box grater.

Green Tomato and Apple Chutney

Makes about 6 to 7 8-oz. (250-mL) jars

A traditional English condiment, this chutney is excellent in a sandwich with any type of meat or cheese. It is a great accompaniment to beef dishes such as meat loaf, scrambled eggs or macaroni and cheese.

1	lemon	1
5 cups	finely chopped green tomatoes	1.2 L
2 cups	finely chopped apples	475 mL
1 cup	finely chopped onions	240 mL
2	cloves garlic, peeled and minced	2
1 cup	currants	240 mL
1 cup	brown sugar	240 mL
1 cup	cider vinegar	240 mL
1 Tbsp.	mustard seeds	15 mL
1½ tsp.	dried chili flakes	7.5 mL
1 tsp.	salt	5 mL
1 tsp.	ginger	5 mL

Prepare the preserving jars.

Slice the lemon very thinly, discarding the ends and seeds. Chop very finely.

Combine all the ingredients in your preserving pot. Simmer over medium heat for 25–30 minutes, or until thickened. Stir often to prevent sticking, especially during the last 10 minutes of cooking time.

Remove from the heat. Spoon the chutney into hot, sterilized jars, leaving ½ inch (1.2 cm) head space. Wipe the rims clean. Seal according to manufacturer's directions. Process the jars in a boiling water bath for 10 minutes.

Ripe Tomato Chutney

Makes about 7 to 8 8-oz. (250-mL) jars

A sweet, spicy accompaniment for any type of meat or a pasta, rice or vegetable casserole. You can even serve it for breakfast, with bacon and eggs.

8 cups	chopped tomatoes	2 L
6 cups	chopped apples	1.5 L
1 cup	chopped onion	240 mL
1 cup	chopped red bell pepper	240 mL
2	cloves garlic, peeled and minced	2
1 cup	red wine vinegar	240 mL
2 cups	brown sugar	475 mL
1 Tbsp.	mustard seeds	15 mL
1½ tsp.	salt	7.5 mL
1 tsp.	each cumin, coriander, cinnamon and chili powder	5 mL

Prepare the preserving jars.

Combine the tomatoes, apples, onion, red pepper, garlic and vinegar in your preserving pot. Bring to a boil over high heat. Reduce the heat to medium and simmer for 30 minutes, stirring occasionally. Stir in the remaining ingredients and simmer for another 30–40 minutes, or until thickened, stirring often.

Remove from the heat. Ladle the chutney into hot, sterilized jars, leaving ½ inch (1.2 cm) head space. Wipe the rims clean. Seal according to manufacturer's directions. Process the jars in a boiling water bath for 10 minutes.

About Cumin

One of the major components of curry powder, cumin is used in chili powder as well. Cumin is available as seeds or powder and has a distinctive warm, sweet flavor that is quite powerful and lasting. Cumin is often paired with coriander.

Spread a little cream
cheese on a toasted
bagel. Top with banana
chutney and crumbled
crisp bacon. Mmm . . .

Banana and Date Chutney

Makes about 5 to 6 8-oz. (250-mL) jars

1 cup	chopped apple	240 mL
1/2 cup	finely chopped onion	120 mL
1 1/2 cups	cider vinegar	360 mL
1/4 cup	lime juice	60 mL
7	medium bananas, ripe but not mushy	7
1 cup	chopped dates	240 mL
1/4 cup	chopped candied ginger	60 mL
1/2 cup	brown sugar	120 mL
1/4 cup	molasses	60 mL
1 tsp.	salt	5 mL
1/2 tsp.	each allspice, curry powder, cayenne pepper and coriander	2.5 mL

Prepare the preserving jars.

Combine the apples, onion, vinegar and lime juice in your preserving pot. Bring to a boil over medium heat and simmer for 10 minutes.

Peel the bananas and chop them into 1/2-inch (1.2-cm) pieces; add them to the pot. Stir in the remaining ingredients. Reduce the heat to medium-low and simmer for about 20 minutes, stirring often, until the mixture is thick and pulpy.

Note: The chutney can become very thick and sticky. You may need to add 1/4– 1/3 cup (60–80 mL) water to prevent the chutney from sticking and to make it easier to fill the jars. Just be sure that the chutney is uniformly hot and bubbling before removing it from the heat. (If you have a suitable non-stick pot, use it for making this chutney.)

Remove from the heat. Spoon the chutney into hot, sterilized jars, leaving ½ inch (1.2 cm) head space. Wipe the rims clean. Seal according to manufacturer's directions. Process the jars in a boiling water bath for 10 minutes.

Curried Apple Chutney

Makes about 7 to 8 8-oz. (250-mL) jars

9 cups	peeled, chopped, cored apples (about 3 lbs./1.4 kg)	2.2 L
2 cups	finely chopped onion	475 mL
2 cups	golden raisins	475 mL
2 cups	brown sugar	475 mL
1½ cups	cider vinegar	360 mL
1 Tbsp.	mustard seeds	15 mL
1½ tsp.	salt	7.5 mL
1 tsp.	dried chili flakes	5 mL
1 tsp.	curry powder	5 mL
½ tsp.	each turmeric, cumin, coriander, cardamom and ginger	2.5 mL

The ultimate chutney with cheese and crackers and a perfect partner for the Cheddar Cheese Ball with Port and Dijon Mustard (page 202).

Prepare the preserving jars.

Combine all the ingredients in your preserving pot. Bring to a boil over medium-high heat, stirring occasionally. Reduce the heat to medium and simmer for 1 – 1½ hours, or until thickened, stirring often. Stir almost constantly during the last 15 – 20 minutes of cooking time to prevent scorching.

Remove from the heat. Ladle the chutney into hot, sterilized jars, leaving ½ inch (1.2 cm) head space. Wipe the rims clean. Seal according to manufacturer's directions. Process the jars in a boiling water bath for 10 minutes.

Rhubarb and Ginger Chutney

Makes about 7 to 8 8-oz. (250-mL) jars

For ginger lovers only! This unusual chutney adds zest to any curried main dish, or for that matter, to a simple snack of bread and cheese.

8 cups	rhubarb cut into ½-inch (1.2-cm) dice	2 L
2 cups	finely chopped onion	475 mL
2	cloves garlic, peeled and minced	2
4 cups	dark brown sugar	950 mL
2 cups	cider vinegar	475 mL
1 cup	golden raisins	240 mL
⅔ cup	grated fresh ginger	160 mL
2 tsp.	salt	10 mL
2 tsp.	mustard seeds	10 mL
1 tsp.	dried chili flakes	5 mL
1 tsp.	allspice	5 mL
1 tsp.	coriander	5 mL
½ tsp.	cinnamon	2.5 mL
½ tsp.	cloves	2.5 mL

Prepare the preserving jars.

Combine all the ingredients in your preserving pot and bring to a boil over medium-high heat, stirring occasionally. Reduce the heat to medium and simmer, stirring often, for 35–45 minutes, until thickened.

Remove from the heat. Ladle the chutney into hot, sterilized jars, leaving ½ inch (1.2 cm) head space. Wipe the rims clean. Seal according to manufacturer's directions. Process the jars in a boiling water bath for 10 minutes.

Blackberry and Apple Chutney

Makes about 4 to 5 8-oz. (250-mL) jars

An elegant preserve brimming with the flavor of ripe blackberries. The perfect complement to pâtés, roast poultry or game.

1	orange, juice and grated zest	1
½ cup	finely chopped onion	120 mL
1 cup	brown sugar	240 mL
½ cup	honey	120 mL
½ cup	red wine vinegar	120 mL
2 cups	blackberries	475 mL
3 cups	peeled, cored, chopped apples	720 mL
½ cup	golden raisins	120 mL
1 tsp.	salt	5 mL
½ tsp.	cloves	2.5 mL
½ tsp.	allspice	2.5 mL

Prepare the preserving jars.

In your preserving pot, combine the orange juice and zest, onion, sugar, honey and red wine vinegar. Bring to a boil over medium heat and simmer 5 minutes, stirring occasionally. Add the remaining ingredients and simmer for 30–35 minutes, stirring often, until the chutney has thickened slightly.

Remove from the heat. Ladle the chutney into hot, sterilized jars, leaving ½ inch (1.2 cm) head space. Wipe the rims clean. Seal according to manufacturer's directions. Process the jars in a boiling water bath for 10 minutes.

About Allspice

The small round, dried fruit of an evergreen tree of the myrtle family, allspice berries look like large peppercorns. This aptly named spice combines the flavors of cinnamon, nutmeg and cloves, with the flavor of cloves predominating. This complex spice blends well with other spices and complements a wide variety of foods, particularly apples, tomatoes and pumpkins. Ground allspice does not store well, as the flavor tends to deteriorate.

Try this intriguing
chutney spooned
over baked squash
or sweet potato.

Pear Chutney

Makes about 5 to 6 8-oz. (250-mL) jars

6 cups	chopped pears	1.5 L
1 cup	chopped apple	240 mL
½ cup	finely chopped onion	120 mL
½ cup	finely chopped red bell pepper	120 mL
¾ cup	dark raisins	180 mL
½ cup	chopped candied ginger	120 mL
2 cups	brown sugar	475 mL
¾ cup	cider vinegar	180 mL
1	lemon, juice and finely grated zest	1
1 Tbsp.	mustard seeds	15 mL
2 tsp.	dried chili flakes	10 mL
1 tsp.	salt	5 mL
½ tsp.	nutmeg	2.5 mL
½ tsp.	cloves	2.5 mL

Prepare the preserving jars.

Combine all the ingredients in your preserving pot. Bring to a boil over medium heat, stirring occasionally. Simmer, stirring often, until the pears are tender and the mixture has thickened, about 1 hour.

Remove from the heat. Ladle the chutney into hot, sterilized jars, leaving ½ inch (1.2 cm) head space. Wipe the rims clean. Seal according to manufacturer's directions. Process the jars in a boiling water bath for 10 minutes.

Ketchups

Subtly sweet and richly flavored, homemade ketchups are versatile sauces that every home preserver should have in his or her repertoire. You'll be forgiven should your mind stray to a grungy bottle of tomato sauce atop a table in a seedy, all-night diner, or perhaps to a sticky bottle lurking in the depths of your own refrigerator. Yes, that may be ketchup to some people, but homemade ketchup encompasses so much more. You don't have to limit yourself to tomatoes — although homemade tomato ketchup is glorious. Simmer up a batch of fruity cranberry or five-fruit ketchup to serve with roast pork, chicken or grilled fish. A robust vegetable ketchup is de rigueur with grilled burgers, of course, but why not try some with rare roast beef, hearty pork or veal chops, or a sizzling steak?

Ketchups bear close resemblance to a couple of characters you are already familiar with — chutneys and fruit butters. Usually highly seasoned, ketchups are made of ingredients similar to those in chutney, but are generally smooth and of a thinner consistency. Juicy, fully ripe fruits are used. The actual preparation of ketchup is more like that of a fruit butter. The fruit and/or vegetables are prepared, aromatic seasonings added and the concoction simmered for about an hour. This evaporation process reduces the sauce to the desired thickness. The ketchup is most often sieved or puréed to velvety smoothness before being bottled. Half-pint (250-mL) jars are recommended, as ketchup is usually used in small quantities.

Ketchup is ready when it has thickened to a — well, a ketchup-like consistency. To test for doneness, simply spoon a little ketchup on a cold plate and chill in the freezer for 2 minutes. Draw your finger through the center; if a clear track remains, the ketchup is done. Should the ketchup become too thick, either during cooking or afterwards in the jar, it can be diluted with a little water, vinegar, or both.

Old-Fashioned Tomato Ketchup

Makes about 5 to 6 8-oz. (250-mL) jars

2	3-inch (7.5-cm) cinnamon sticks, broken	2
1 tsp.	whole cloves	5 mL
1 tsp.	whole allspice	5 mL
2 Tbsp.	mustard seeds	30 mL
1 tsp.	celery seeds	5 mL
10 lbs.	ripe tomatoes, preferably plum or Roma	4.5 kg
1 cup	chopped onion	240 mL
1 cup	chopped red or green bell peppers	240 mL
1½ cups	cider vinegar	360 mL
1 cup	brown sugar	240 mL
1½ Tbsp.	salt	22.5 mL

This hearty, homemade version beats store-bought any day. Stir a little into gravy or savory sauces for an extra zing.

Certain modern varieties of tomatoes can vary considerably in acidity. In order to safely process tomato-based foods such as salsa, chili sauce or ketchup in a boiling water bath, it is essential to add lemon juice or vinegar to compensate for any lack of natural acid.

Coarsely chop the tomatoes. Combine the tomatoes, onion and peppers in your preserving pot. Bring to a boil over medium heat and simmer for 30 minutes, stirring occasionally. Remove from the heat. Press the pulp through a sieve or food mill.

Put the cinnamon sticks, cloves, allspice, mustard and celery seeds into a cheesecloth bag and tie the top with string.

Return the pulp to the pot and add the remaining ingredients. Prepare the preserving jars. Simmer the sauce about 1 hour, until thickened, stirring often. (Stir constantly during the last 15–20 minutes to prevent scorching.)

Remove from the heat. Discard the spice bag. Pour the ketchup into hot, sterilized jars, leaving ½ inch (1.2 cm) head space. Wipe the rims clean. Seal according to manufacturer's directions. Process the jars in a boiling water bath for 15 minutes.

Chili sauce is a lot like
ketchup, only chunkier.
It is highly compatible
with barbecued meats
or poultry and terrific
with savory meat pies.

Country Style Chili Sauce

Makes about 5 to 6 pint (500-mL) jars

10 cups	chopped tomatoes, preferably plum or Roma	2.4 L
3 cups	chopped onions	720 mL
2 cups	chopped red bell peppers	475 mL
1½ cups	chopped celery	360 mL
3	small chili peppers, seeded and minced	3
2	cloves garlic, minced	2
1½ cups	cider vinegar	360 mL
1 cup	brown sugar	240 mL
2½ tsp.	salt	12.5 mL
½ tsp.	ground black pepper	2.5 mL
½ tsp.	dry English mustard	2.5 mL
½ tsp.	celery seed	2.5 mL
½ tsp.	cloves	2.5 mL
½ tsp.	allspice	2.5 mL
½ tsp.	cinnamon	2.5 mL
½ tsp.	ginger	2.5 mL

Prepare the preserving jars.

Combine all the ingredients except the spices in your preserving pot. Bring to a boil over medium-high heat. Reduce the heat to medium and simmer, stirring often, for 1 hour. Stir in the spices, and continue to cook the sauce until it reaches a consistency that is slightly thicker than ketchup. This may take 1–1½ hours. You can test for doneness by placing a little sauce on a cold plate. When the plate is tilted, very little liquid should ooze away from the solids. Once the cooking is complete, taste the sauce and adjust the seasoning to suit your taste, adding a little more vinegar, sugar, spices or some liquid hot sauce, if desired. You may need to cook the sauce a little longer if you add additional vinegar.

Remove from the heat. Ladle the sauce into hot, sterilized jars, leaving ½ inch (1.2 cm) head space. Wipe the rims clean. Seal according to manufacturer's directions. Process the jars in a boiling water bath for 15 minutes.

About Peeling and Seeding Tomatoes

There are two schools of thought on the subject of peeling tomatoes. Many cooks shudder at the very idea of using unpeeled tomatoes. Others believe that tomato skins contribute a stronger, richer flavor to their recipes.

I don't mind eating tomato skins, and I can't say that I've ever noticed a difference in taste one way or the other. To me, peeling tomatoes is not a necessity. But for those times when you want to peel and seed your tomatoes, here's how to do it.

Bring a large pot of water to a boil. Using a sharp paring knife, remove the cores from the tomatoes and make a small X at the base of each one.

Working with just a few tomatoes at a time, carefully place the tomatoes in the boiling water and leave them there for 30 to 60 seconds.

Remove the tomatoes with a slotted spoon, and transfer them to a big bowl of cold water. After a few minutes, they will be cool enough to handle, and the skins will slide right off.

Cut the tomatoes in half crosswise, gently squeeze out the seeds and the juice, then chop them for your recipes.

Five-Fruit Ketchup

Makes about 6 to 7 8-oz. (250-mL) jars

Savor summer's finest fruits in this mellow, richly flavored ketchup. Serve with pâtés, cold sliced meats or cheese and crackers.

2	3-inch (7.5-cm) cinnamon sticks	2
1 tsp.	whole cloves	5 mL
1 tsp.	whole allspice berries	5 mL
1 tsp.	black peppercorns	5 mL
1 tsp.	mustard seeds	5 mL
6 cups	chopped tomatoes	1.5 L
2 cups	each chopped peaches, apples, pears and plums	475 mL
1 cup	chopped onion	240 mL
2	cloves garlic, minced	2
2	jalapeño peppers, seeded and finely chopped	2
2 cups	cider vinegar	475 mL
2 cups	brown sugar	475 mL
2 tsp.	salt	10 mL

Put the cinnamon sticks, cloves, allspice, peppercorns and mustard seeds in a cheesecloth bag and tie the top with string.

Combine all the ingredients in your preserving pot. Bring to a boil over medium-high heat. Reduce the heat to medium and simmer for about 1 hour, stirring frequently. Remove from the heat. Discard the spice bag. Press the mixture through a sieve or food mill, then return it to the pot. Return to a boil and when the ketchup is uniformly hot and bubbling, remove from the heat.

Pour the sauce into hot, sterilized jars, leaving ½ inch (1.2 cm) head space. Wipe the rims clean. Seal according to manufacturer's directions. Process the jars in a boiling water bath for 15 minutes.

Cranberry Ketchup

Makes about 6 to 7 8-oz. (250-mL) jars

2 cups	chopped red onion	475 mL
2	oranges, juice and finely grated zest	2
3 cups	water	720 mL
8 cups	cranberries (about 2 lbs./900 g)	2 L
1 cup	red wine vinegar	240 mL
2 cups	brown sugar	475 mL
1 tsp.	each cloves, cinnamon, allspice and ginger	5 mL
1 tsp.	salt	5 mL
1/2 tsp.	pepper	2.5 mL

A gorgeous, ruby-red sauce with a lively flavor, this is an excellent companion to rich entrées such as roast duck, goose or venison. Cranberries are very rich in pectin, so the ketchup may thicken up faster than you expect. If it should become too thick, add a little water or orange juice to thin it down. Be careful not to add too much; start with about 1/4 cup (60 mL).

Prepare the preserving jars.

Combine the onion, orange juice and zest and water in your preserving pot. Bring to a boil over medium heat and simmer, covered, for about 10 minutes, until the onion is tender. Add the cranberries, cover and cook for another 10–15 minutes, stirring occasionally, until the cranberries burst.

Remove from the heat and pass the mixture through a sieve or food mill. Return the puréed mixture to the pot and stir in the remaining ingredients. Bring to a boil, stirring constantly. As soon as the mixture is bubbling and heated through, remove from the heat and immediately pour into hot, sterilized jars, leaving 1/4 inch (.6 cm) head space. Wipe the rims clean. Seal according to manufacturer's directions. Process the jars in a boiling water bath for 15 minutes.

Feisty Red Pepper Ketchup

Makes about 5 to 6 8-oz. (250-mL) jars

You can also use brightly colored yellow or orange peppers for this stylish sauce, but stay away from green ones—they do not produce an attractive ketchup. This ketchup will not be perfectly smooth. If you would like it that way, pass it through a sieve or food mill after it is removed from the heat. Return the ketchup to the pot, heat to boiling and fill the jars as usual.

2 Tbsp.	mustard seeds	30 mL
1 Tbsp.	black peppercorns	15 mL
1 Tbsp.	coriander seeds	15 mL
1 tsp.	whole cloves	5 mL
3 lbs.	red bell peppers, cored and seeded	1.4 kg
3	onions, peeled	3
2	apples, peeled and cored	2
3	small hot red chilies	3
2 cups	red wine vinegar	475 mL
3/4 cup	brown sugar	180 mL
2 Tbsp.	prepared creamed horseradish	30 mL
2 tsp.	pickling salt	10 mL
1	lemon, zest only, cut off in a continuous spiral	1

Put the mustard seeds, black peppercorns, coriander seeds and cloves in a cheesecloth bag and tie the top with string.

Cut the peppers, onions and apples into chunks. Place in the bowl of a food processor along with the chilies. Process until very finely ground. Transfer to your preserving pot.

Prepare the preserving jars.

Add the remaining ingredients and the cheesecloth bag of spices to the preserving pot and bring to a boil over high heat. Reduce the heat to medium and simmer, stirring occasionally, for 45–60 minutes, until thickened.

Remove from the heat. Discard the lemon zest and spice bag. Pour into hot, sterilized jars, leaving ½ inch (1.2 cm) head space. Wipe the rims clean. Seal according to manufacturer's directions. Process the jars in a boiling water bath for 15 minutes.

Infused
Vinegars

Specialty food shops often have gorgeous displays of imported herb and fruit vinegars. If you've ever longed to purchase such vinegars, but have found them to be too expensive, you will be delighted to discover how easily and inexpensively they can be made at home.

No specialized equipment is required, just a little time and patience. Any recycled or purchased bottles will do, as long as they are properly prepared and can be sealed with plastic caps or corks.

Flavored vinegars are known as infused vinegars. An infused vinegar is a vinegar that has been steeped with a flavoring such as herbs, spices, fruit or flowers for a period of time, allowing the vinegar to take on the flavors of the other ingredients.

Do not confuse infusing vinegars with actually making vinegar. Vinegar is a solution of acetic acid and water. Making vinegar is a natural process that occurs if you allow a sweet liquid to undergo fermentation. The sugar in the liquid is first converted to alcohol by yeasts, and then the alcohol is eventually converted to acetic acid by bacteria. Certain conditions must exist to allow fermentation to occur.

Infusing vinegar is a much simpler process that begins with good-quality ready-made white or red wine vinegar. Mellow-flavored cider vinegar is also a good choice, especially for fruit vinegars, where color is not an issue. Do not be tempted to use regular white distilled vinegar; it is a little too harsh for this purpose. Mild wine or cider vinegars readily absorb delicate herb and fruit flavors.

Blending Flavors

The flavors of infused vinegars mellow and blend in the bottle, so you can use virtually any combination of flavorings and get a good result. Infused vinegars offer plenty of room for creativity and experimentation. Satisfy your urge to be innovative by blending finished vinegars together like wines to create new and unexpected combinations that are definitely not garden variety.

As an acid, vinegar reacts with metal ions from the surface of aluminum, copper, iron or zinc-lined vessels. Never steep vinegar in metal containers—the chemical reaction will cause undesirable flavors to develop. You can also discolor your pots. Use glass or ceramic containers to steep vinegars, and heat them only in stainless steel or enamel-lined pots.

Old or new, bottles for vinegar must be absolutely clean. Put them through the dishwasher, then boil them for 15 minutes to sterilize them. Dry the bottles on their sides on a baking sheet in a warm oven, about 150°F (65°C), until there is no sign of moisture inside.

Stoppering the Bottles

Seal bottles of vinegar using either plastic screw-top caps or corks. Metal screw-tops are fine for short-term storage but may corrode if the vinegar is kept for long periods.

Corks are a practical and aesthetically pleasing choice for stoppering bottled vinegars. Never use recycled corks, which can lead to spoilage. New corks are inexpensive and are usually available from cookware or wine-making supply stores. Try to find tapered corks if you can; they are much easier to work with.

Simmer the corks in a covered pot for 15 minutes just prior to use. The heat will kill any microorganisms that might be present and will also soften the corks, making it easier to insert them into the bottles.

Push the cork into the bottle as far as you can manually, then use a wooden mallet or similar tool to gently tap the cork in as far as it will go. Any cork protruding over the rim of the bottle can be trimmed neatly off with a sharp knife, if desired.

Infused vinegars are not heat processed, as the vinegar itself is a preservative. The acidity of full-strength vinegar is too high to allow the growth of microorganisms, as long as proper sanitary procedures have been followed.

Sealing Bottles with Wax

The final step is to seal and protect the bottles with wax, to keep them airtight.

The hard, glossy coating that you see on fancy, gourmet bottles sold in shops is proper sealing wax. It is rather expensive and difficult to come by, and is really better saved for decorative applications only (see "Gifts from the Pantry").

Simple paraffin wax can be purchased from grocery or hardware stores and will do a very satisfactory job. It can be colored by melting an old candle stub (unscented) or crayon along with the paraffin.

I like to use a mixture of paraffin and beeswax, about half and half. This is primarily for aesthetic reasons — beeswax has a delightful scent and a lovely golden color that is most attractive. Beeswax can often be found at craft stores, but I buy mine from a shop that sells honey and beekeeping supplies.

You need an old pot or a small metal container in which to melt the wax. Once used, this container is pretty much dedicated to the purpose of melting wax. I use a small pot that I bought at a garage sale. I leave the wax to harden after each use, then just wrap the whole thing in a plastic bag and it's ready for next time. A clean tin can works well too.

Chop up the wax and place it in the metal container, then place the container in a pot of water that is simmering (not boiling) over low heat. The melted wax needs to be deep enough so that it will cover part of the neck of the bottle. The bottles and corks must be completely dry. Dip the top of the bottle repeatedly into the melted wax, allowing the wax to set between applications. (Setting only takes a minute or two, if that.) Several coats of wax are needed to give an attractive and effective seal.

Basic Herb Vinegar

▶ Rinse the herbs briefly under running water or swish them in a sinkful of water. Do not soak the herbs for a long time.

▶ Drain the herbs in a colander, then gently roll them in a towel to blot up moisture or spin them in a salad spinner.

▶ Leave the herbs to air-dry for at least an hour. There must be no water clinging to the leaves.

▶ Trim the herbs if necessary, removing coarse stem ends, flower buds and any withered or insect-eaten leaves.

▶ Place the herbs in a clean, dry, sterilized jar. A wide-mouthed glass jar that narrows slightly at the top is best — that is, a jar that has shoulders, not one that is straight up and down. This will help keep the herbs covered with the vinegar.

▶ The herbs should fill the jar two-thirds to three-quarters full. The basic ratio is about 1 cup (240 mL) of loosely packed herbs to about 2 cups (475 mL) of vinegar, but this is not a hard and fast rule.

Suggested Uses for Herb Vinegars

Aromatic herb vinegars can be used almost anywhere you would use regular vinegar.

▶ Use it in vinaigrettes—to dress salads of greens, vegetables, pasta, grains, poultry or fish.

▶ Splash it on steamed vegetables to liven them up.

▶ Try it in potato salad—it's terrific!

▶ Use it in any kind of marinade to tenderize and add interesting flavors.

▶ Make a delicately flavored herb mayonnaise.

▶ Add a dash to give flavor and interest to reduced-salt recipes.

▶ Make quick "pickled" vegetables by marinating cucumber, tomato or carrot slices or mushrooms in herb vinegars.

- Fill the jar with vinegar to a maximum of 1 inch (2.5 cm) below the rim of the jar. The herbs must be completely immersed in the vinegar — you may need to trim longer sprigs or poke the herbs down below the surface. Mold can develop if the herbs are exposed.

- Cover the vinegar tightly. If the jar has a metal lid, cover the mouth of the jar with plastic wrap first.

- Place the vinegar in a sunny spot where you will remember to shake or stir it once or twice a week. The warmth will speed up the decomposition of the herbs, drawing out the aromatic oils more quickly.

- Let the vinegar steep for 2 to 4 weeks. Some vinegars will be ready more quickly than others. You can sniff and taste the vinegar after 10 days or so to see if the flavor has developed to your liking. If it has, proceed to the next step. If not, let it steep for a longer period. The flavors will intensify with time, but after about 4 weeks the flavors will pretty much have been extracted from the herbs.

- Strain the vinegar through a sieve lined with a double thickness of dampened cheesecloth. The cheesecloth is dampened first so it doesn't absorb a lot of the vinegar.

- In a non-reactive pot, gently heat the vinegar just to a simmer.

- Remove from the heat and strain a second time through clean cheesecloth.

- Using a funnel, carefully pour the vinegar into clean, dry, sterilized bottles.

- Place clean, dry fresh herb sprigs in the bottles if desired, for decoration and identification.

- Cover loosely with cheesecloth and leave the vinegar to cool.

- Seal the bottles by capping with plastic screw-tops or corks. Complete the seal by dipping the tops of the bottles in melted wax.

- Label the bottles, listing the types of herbs and the date, and store them in a cool, dark place. Herb vinegars will keep almost indefinitely but are at their best if used within 6 months—a year at the most.

- Once the vinegar is opened, remove and discard the herbs. They may become moldy once they are exposed to the air.

Some Suggested Flavorings for Herb Vinegars

- thyme, savory, marjoram with red wine vinegar

- rosemary, garlic, hot chili pepper with red wine vinegar

- rosemary, orange zest with red wine vinegar

- oregano, shallot, hot chili pepper with red wine vinegar

- mint, grapefruit zest with white wine vinegar

- mint, dill, lime zest with white wine vinegar

- dill, lemon zest, fennel seeds with white wine vinegar

Using Garlic or Shallots for Additional Flavor

Garlic or shallots can be added to any herb vinegar for additional flavor. This is done at the time the vinegar is heated, just prior to bottling.

Select small cloves of garlic and/or the tiniest shallots. Shallots will need to be halved or quartered to fit through the opening of the bottle. Add the garlic or shallots to the vinegar in the pot, heat gently to simmering, then strain. Place the garlic or shallots in the bottle, then proceed as usual.

You can also thread the garlic or shallots onto a bamboo skewer for a decorative look. The skewer should be about three-quarters the length of the bottle you are using. Soak the skewer in water beforehand; otherwise it will float to the top of the bottle.

Basic Fruit Vinegar

- ▸ Allow 3–4 lbs. (1.4–1.8 kg) of fruit for each 4 cups (950 mL) of vinegar. Use fruit that is fully ripe.

- ▸ Rinse or wash the fruit briefly. Do not allow it to soak in water for a long time.

- ▸ Drain the fruit thoroughly in a colander, then gently blot it dry using paper towels.

- ▸ Sort the fruit, discarding any that is damaged or moldy. (It is fine to use bruised fruit as long as the bruises are completely cut away.)

- ▸ It is not necessary to stem currants, hull strawberries or pit cherries. Likewise, you do not need to peel or pit peaches or plums, but larger fruit should be cut into approximately ½-inch (1.2-cm) pieces.

- ▸ Place the fruit in a bowl and crush it with a potato masher to release the juices.

- ▸ In a non-reactive pot, heat the vinegar gently, just to a simmer. Remove from the heat, let it cool slightly, then stir in the prepared fruit.

- ▸ Cover the pot loosely with a clean dish towel and let stand until it is completely cool.

- ▸ Transfer the mixture to a clean, dry, sterilized jar, and cover tightly. A wide-mouthed jar that narrows slightly at the top is best. This will help keep the fruit covered with the vinegar. If the jar has a metal lid, cover the mouth of the jar with plastic wrap first.

- ▸ Store in a cool, dark place for at least one month. Stir the vinegar three or four times a week. Taste the vinegar after one month—it should have a rich, full, fruit flavor. If you are not satisfied with the intensity of the flavor, leave it to steep for another 2 weeks.

- When the vinegar is ready, pour it into a dampened jelly bag suspended over a bowl and allow it to drip through overnight. (You can also use a sieve lined with a double thickness of cheesecloth.) Discard the drained fruit.

- Pour the vinegar into a large, non-reactive pot. The wider the pot is, the better. The vinegar should be no more than 4 inches (10 cm) deep to allow it to come to a boil very quickly. The rapid boiling preserves the rich color of the vinegar. If necessary, boil the vinegar in several batches.

- If desired, the vinegar can be sweetened slightly with sugar. Add 1–1½ Tbsp. (15–22.5 mL) for each 1 cup (240 mL) of vinegar.

Suggested Uses for Fruit Vinegars

- Team fruit vinegars with delicate salad oils in vinaigrette dressings. Fruit vinegars are especially delightful with nut-flavored oils such as hazelnut or pistachio.

- Replace the lemon juice in many recipes with fruit vinegar—for example, in dressings for fruit salads.

- Use fruit vinegar to deglaze the pan when preparing sautéed veal or chicken to make a tart, fruity sauce.

- Use fruit vinegars in marinades to tenderize and add flavor to pork, veal or poultry.

- Sprinkle fruit vinegar and sugar over fresh berries.

- Mix fruit vinegar with an equal amount of honey to make a tart sauce for fresh fruit.

- Use it to add a sweet-tart flavor to preserves, stewed fruit or fruit sauces and purees.

- Make a refreshing, old-fashioned fruit drink known as a shrub — stir fruit vinegar into club soda, and add ice and sugar to taste.

- Quickly bring the vinegar to a boil over high heat. Boil for 3 minutes.

- Skim off any foam and allow the vinegar to cool. Strain the vinegar a second time, discarding any sediment. Bottle and seal as for herb vinegar.

- Label the sealed bottles with the type of fruit and the date and store the vinegar in a cool, dark place.

- Although the flavor of fruit vinegar improves with age, colors may eventually fade or darken. Fruit vinegars often develop a fine sediment, which, though unattractive, is harmless. Simply decant the vinegar through a dampened coffee filter or cheesecloth into another bottle.

- Fruit vinegars will keep almost indefinitely if they are properly prepared and stored, but it is recommended to use them within 6 months, or a year at the most.

Some Suggested Flavorings for Fruit Vinegars

Many fruits can be used to make fruit vinegars, including strawberries, blackberries, raspberries, blueberries, cherries, currants, peaches, apricots, pears and plums.

You can also combine fruits with herbs, spices or citrus zests for extra-special flavors.

- blueberry, mint with red wine vinegar

- cranberry, orange zest with red wine vinegar

- blackberry, lemon balm with red wine vinegar

- peach, ginger with white wine vinegar

- strawberry, lime zest with white wine vinegar

- pear, rosemary with red wine vinegar

Lovely Lavender Vinegar

Makes 2 cups (475 mL)

Delectably different in a vinaigrette, or try a splash over fresh strawberries or ripe melon.

| 8 | large-headed stalks of fresh lavender | 8 |
| 2 cups | white wine vinegar | 475 mL |

Briefly swish the lavender in a bowl of salted water to get rid of any insects. Rinse in clear water, shake dry, then blot with paper towels. Trim the stalks if necessary to fit your bottle — the lavender should stand about three-quarters as high.

Place the lavender in a clean, dry, sterilized, wide-mouthed jar.

Heat the vinegar just to a simmer, then remove from the heat and let it cool slightly. Pour the vinegar into the jar, ensuring the lavender is completely covered. Cover and leave it to stand in a sunny spot for 2 to 3 weeks, giving the bottle a slight shake occasionally.

Strain the vinegar through a sieve lined with dampened cheesecloth. In a non-reactive pot, gently heat the vinegar just to a simmer, then strain it a second time. Cover loosely with cheesecloth and allow the vinegar to cool to room temperature. Carefully pour vinegar into 1 or 2 clean, dry, sterilized bottles. If you like, place one or two stalks of fresh lavender in the bottles before sealing. Cap or stop the bottles with corks. Seal with wax.

Previous page, foreground: *Cranberry Christmas Vinegar (p. 192)*, background, from left to right: *Hot Chili Pepper Vinegar (p. 193)*, *Raspberry Vinegar (p. 191)*, *Dill, lemon zest and fennel seeds with white wine vinegar (p. 183)*.

Facing page: *A selection of decorating ideas from Gifts from the Pantry (pp. 218-224)*.

Opal Basil Vinegar

Makes 4 cups (950 mL)

2 cups	rinsed and dried opal basil, lightly packed	475 mL
4 cups	white wine vinegar	950 mL

A tender annual, aromatic basil may well be the most popular of culinary herbs. Basil is available in many varieties, including anise basil, lemon basil, cinnamon basil and the star of this recipe, opal basil. Opal basil has a warm, spicy fragrance and slightly peppery flavor with overtones of clove and nutmeg. Its beautiful dark purple leaves give the vinegar a rich jewel-toned hue.

Gently bruise the basil in your hands to release the fragrant oils. Place the basil into a dry, sterilized wide-mouthed jar. Pour the vinegar over the herbs, making sure they are completely covered. Cover and steep for 2 to 3 weeks, stirring once or twice a week.

Strain the vinegar through a sieve lined with dampened cheesecloth.

In a non-reactive pot, gently heat the vinegar just to a simmer, then strain it a second time. Cover loosely with cheesecloth and allow the vinegar to cool to room temperature.

Carefully pour the vinegar into clean, dry, sterilized bottles, using a funnel. If you like, add some fresh basil to each bottle before sealing. Cap or stop the bottles with corks. Seal with wax.

Scarborough Fair Vinegar

Makes 4 cups (950 mL)

2 cups	equal amounts of rinsed and dried parsley, sage, rosemary and thyme, lightly packed	475 mL
4 cups	red wine vinegar	950 mL

This pungent blend of gardeners' favorite herbs and red wine vinegar is an excellent multipurpose vinegar to have on hand in the pantry for vinaigrettes and marinades.

Place the herbs in a clean, dry, sterilized wide-mouthed jar. Pour the vinegar over the herbs, making sure they are completely covered. Cover and steep for 2 to 3 weeks, stirring once or twice a week.

Strain the vinegar through a sieve lined with dampened cheesecloth.

In a non-reactive pot, gently heat the vinegar just to a simmer, then strain it a second time. Cover loosely with cheesecloth and allow the vinegar to cool to room temperature.

Carefully pour the vinegar into clean, dry, sterilized bottles, using a funnel. If you like, add a couple of sprigs of fresh herbs to each bottle before sealing. Cap or stop the bottles with corks. Seal with wax.

Flavoring Vinegars with Fresh Ginger

Fresh ginger adds an exciting dimension to infused vinegars and can complement a variety of herbs or fruits.

Simply add about 2 oz. (57 g) of peeled fresh ginger, cut into 1/4-inch (.6-cm) slices, to every 4 cups (950 mL) of vinegar, during the initial steeping process. Strain the ginger out before bottling.

French Tarragon Vinegar

Makes about 4 cups (950 mL)

2 cups	rinsed and dried French tarragon, lightly packed	475 mL
4 cups	white wine vinegar	950 mL

Place the tarragon into a dry, sterilized, wide-mouthed jar. Pour the vinegar over the herbs, making sure they are completely covered.

Cover and steep for 3 to 4 weeks, stirring once or twice a week.

Strain the vinegar through a sieve lined with dampened cheesecloth.

In a non-reactive pot, gently heat the vinegar just to a simmer, then strain it a second time. Cover loosely with cheesecloth and allow the vinegar to cool to room temperature.

Carefully pour the vinegar into clean, dry, sterilized bottles, using a funnel. If you like, add a couple of sprigs of fresh tarragon to each bottle before sealing. Cap or stop the bottles with corks. Seal with wax.

Tarragon has a pronounced aroma and flavor slightly suggestive of licorice. Nothing can match the flavor of true French tarragon. Other varieties are considerably inferior in flavor. French tarragon is only propagated by root division or from cuttings taken in early summer. Accept no imitations!

Raspberry Vinegar

Makes about 6 cups (1.5 L)

| 3 – 4 lbs. | fresh raspberries, fully ripe | 1.4 – 1.8 kg |
| 4 cups | white wine vinegar | 950 mL |

Rinse and sort the raspberries. Pat them dry with paper towels. Place them in a large bowl and crush gently with a potato masher.

In a non-reactive pot, gently heat the vinegar just to a simmer. Remove from the heat and let it cool slightly. Stir in the raspberries. Cover the pot with a clean dish towel and let stand until completely cool.

Transfer the mixture to a clean, dry, sterilized jar. Cover tightly and store in a cool, dark place for about a month.

When the vinegar is ready, pour it into a dampened jelly bag suspended over a bowl and let it drip through overnight. (You can also use a sieve lined with a double thickness of cheesecloth.)

The next day, discard the berries and place the vinegar in a large, non-reactive pot. Quickly bring it to a boil over high heat. Boil for 3 minutes. Remove from the heat. Skim off any foam that may have occurred. Strain the vinegar a second time. Cover loosely with cheesecloth. When the vinegar has cooled, pour it into clean, dry, sterilized bottles. Cap or stop the bottles with a cork. Seal with wax.

This blush-red vinegar is the most popular of all fruit vinegars. Its slightly sweet flavor and divine color make it indispensable for all kinds of recipes.

Cranberry Christmas Vinegar

Makes 1½–2 cups (360–475 mL)

In this recipe, the fruit, spices and vinegar are steeped in the bottle. The result is a festive-looking, intriguingly flavored infused vinegar, perfect for Christmas gift-giving. The recipe is for one 12–16 oz. (360–475 mL) bottle of vinegar. Simply multiply to make a larger quantity.

½–¾ cup	cranberries	120 – 180 mL
1 tsp.	whole cloves	5 mL
1	3-inch (7.5-cm) cinnamon stick	1
1½–2 cups	cider vinegar	360 – 475 mL
6	dried apricots	6
1	orange, zest only	1
1	6- to 8-inch (15- to 20-cm) sprig fresh mint, rinsed and dried	1

Note: Use the smaller amounts of cranberries and vinegar for smaller bottles.

For each jar soak one bamboo skewer in water. Measure the skewers against your bottles — the skewers should be about ¾ as long as the bottles — break a little off if necessary.

Rinse the cranberries and pat dry with paper towels.

In a non-reactive pot, combine the cranberries, cloves, cinnamon stick and vinegar and heat gently until just barely simmering. Do not boil. Remove from the heat and let cool completely.

Strain the mixture through a sieve, reserving the vinegar. Place the berries and spices in a clean, dry sterilized bottle. If you are making more than one bottle, divide the berries and spices evenly between them.

Carefully thread the apricots onto the skewer. Remember, the apricots have to fit through the opening of the bottle — if they are too big you may need to trim them. Make sure that you don't choose a bottle with a neck that's really narrow — you'll go crazy trying to get the apricots inside.

Place the skewer of apricots, the orange zest and a sprig of mint in the bottle. Using a funnel, pour the vinegar into the bottle, ensuring that all the ingredients are covered. Cap or seal with a cork. Let steep 2 to 3 weeks before using. This vinegar should be used within 3 – 4 months once the bottle has been opened. Remove and discard the fruit and spices as they will mold if exposed to air.

Hot Chili Pepper Vinegar

Makes about 4 cups (950 mL)

3 – 4	hot chili peppers, preferably red (see "Handling Hot Peppers," page 118)	3 – 4
4 cups	cider vinegar	950 mL

Using a paring knife, make 2 or 3 small slits in each pepper. In a non-reactive pot, gently heat the vinegar just to a simmer.

Remove from the heat. Add the peppers and let cool slightly.

Transfer the peppers to clean, dry, sterilized bottles. Using a funnel, pour in the vinegar. Cover loosely and allow the vinegar to cool to room temperature. Cap or stop with a cork. Seal with wax.

I like to find a really gorgeous bottle and pack it full of hot chili peppers. For an even more flavorful vinegar, add a big bushy sprig of rosemary and some juicy cloves of fresh garlic. The peppers can be chopped up and used in cooking, if desired.

Spiced Plum Vinegar

Makes about 6 cups (1.5 L)

This vinegar adds a spicy, fruity tartness to vinaigrette dressings for green salads, fruit salads or sauces for chicken or veal.

3 lbs.	plums, any kind	1.4 kg
5 cups	red wine vinegar	1.2 L
¼ – ⅓ cup	mixed whole spices (broken cinnamon sticks, allspice, cloves, juniper berries, peppercorns, mustard seeds, star anise) tied in a cheesecloth bag	60 – 80 mL

Cut the plums into ½-inch (1.2-cm) pieces, discard the pits and place the plums in a large bowl. Crush with a potato masher.

In a non-reactive pot, gently heat the vinegar and spice bag just to a simmer. Remove from the heat. Let it cool slightly, then stir in the plums. Cover the pot loosely with a clean dish towel and allow to cool completely. Transfer the mixture to a clean, dry, sterilized jar. Cover the jar tightly and store it in a cool, dark place for at least a month. Stir the mixture 3 or 4 times a week.

When the flavor has developed to your satisfaction, transfer the mixture to a dampened jelly bag suspended over a bowl and let it drip through overnight. (You can also use a sieve lined with a double thickness of cheesecloth.)

The next day, discard the plums and place the vinegar in a large non-reactive pot. Quickly bring it to a boil over high heat. Boil for 3 minutes. Remove from the heat. Skim off any foam that may have occurred. Strain the vinegar a second time. Cover loosely with cheesecloth and allow to cool to room temperature. Pour into clean, dry, sterilized bottles. Cap or stop the bottles with a cork. Seal with wax.

Cooking
with Preserves

When you preserve fruits and vegetables in season you are establishing a well-stocked larder of ready-made condiments fit to embellish any meal, from the simplest to the most elegant.

Preserves can also be used as ingredients in a variety of recipes from appetizers to desserts. They can be the inspiration for exotic sauces and glazes or intriguing salad dressings. Relishes and chutneys can be made into dips; and jams, butters and jellies can turn up in muffins, cookies and cakes. Fruit sauces, preserves and conserves can be indispensable in creating elaborate desserts like cheesecakes, trifles or crêpes.

What follows are some imaginative suggestions to start you thinking about your preserves in a whole new way. Think of them as homemade convenience foods! Once you put your mind to it, you will be bursting with ideas for incorporating them into tried and true recipes or using them to invent new ones.

About Vinaigrettes

The word "vinaigrette" is derived from the French word for vinegar — *vinaigre.*

Vinaigrettes are simply oil and vinegar dressings. They can be used to dress fresh greens or salads of cold vegetables, grains or fish. Many vinaigrettes make terrific marinades for grilled meats, poultry, fish or vegetables.

Vinaigrettes can be a lifesaver to have on hand in the refrigerator, where they will easily keep for months. You can also make them up fresh in just a few minutes using your own infused vinegars and a good-quality salad oil. Experiment with the proportions of oil and vinegar until you find one that is right for you. Plan on about 2 Tbsp. (30 mL) of vinaigrette per serving on salads.

Mayonnaise Flavored with Fruit Vinegar

Makes about 2½ cups (600 mL)

1	egg	1
2	egg yolks	2
2 tsp.	Dijon mustard	10 mL
¼ cup	fruit vinegar, your choice	60 mL
2 cups	canola oil	475 mL
	salt and freshly ground black pepper to taste	

Beat the egg, egg yolks, mustard and vinegar to combine, using a whisk, food processor or blender.

Gradually add the oil, drop by drop at first, then in a slow, steady stream, beating all the while. Season with salt and pepper.

Fruit-flavored mayonnaise may be used as a dressing for chicken, turkey or fruit salads. Thinned with additional vinegar, it makes a delightful sauce for cold poached chicken breasts or grilled salmon.

Basic Fruit Vinaigrette

Makes about 1½ cups (360 mL)

½ cup	fruit vinegar, your choice	120 mL
½ cup	olive oil	120 mL
½ cup	canola oil	120 mL
1 Tbsp.	sugar	15 mL
	salt and freshly ground black pepper to taste	

Whisk all ingredients together in a small bowl. Refrigerate until ready to use. Whisk again before pouring over the salad greens.

This will keep for weeks in the refrigerator.

Fruit vinaigrette is delightful on a summer salad of fresh mixed greens, such as endive, spinach, radicchio and red leaf lettuce. Toss in some sliced fresh fruit or berries just before serving. I like to add a little crumbled fresh goat's cheese.

Creamy Herb and Garlic Dip or Salad Dressing

Makes about 1 cup (240 mL)

Serve this with raw vegetables as a dip or thin with a little milk to use as a salad dressing. You can use a large, hollowed-out red bell pepper to hold the dip. Trim a thin slice from the bottom of the pepper, if necessary, to even it out and make it stand upright.

½ cup	mayonnaise	120 mL
½ cup	sour cream or yogurt	120 mL
2 Tbsp.	herbal vinegar, your choice	30 mL
2 Tbsp.	finely chopped fresh herbs, your choice	30 mL
½ tsp.	sugar	2.5 mL
	salt and freshly ground black pepper to taste	

Whisk all the ingredients together in a small bowl. Refrigerate for 3 – 4 hours to blend the flavors.

Curried Chutney Dip

Makes about 1¼ cups (300 mL)

Serve this fast and fabulous dip with sliced unpeeled red apples and pears. Sprinkle the fruit with a little lemon juice to prevent browning. Any kind of chutney may be used; Pineapple and Papaya Chutney (page 156) is especially nice.

1 cup	sour cream or yogurt	240 mL
3 Tbsp.	chutney (pages 154 to 168)	45 mL
2 Tbsp.	finely chopped candied ginger	30 mL
2 Tbsp.	curry powder	30 mL

Combine all the ingredients in a small bowl. Cover and refrigerate for at least 1 hour to blend the flavors. Serve in a small crock or decorative serving dish.

Cucumber and Dill Pickle Dip

Makes about 2½ cups (600 mL)

1 cup	finely diced, peeled cucumbers	240 mL
2	Simply Good Dill Pickles, finely chopped (page 123)	2
¼ cup	finely chopped green onions	60 mL
1 Tbsp.	red wine herb vinegar, such as Scarborough Fair Vinegar (page 189)	15 mL
½ cup	sour cream or yogurt	120 mL
½ cup	mayonnaise	120 mL
1 Tbsp.	chopped fresh dill (optional)	15 mL

Discard the cucumber seeds if the cucumber is especially seedy; if you're using English cucumbers, don't worry about it.

Mix all the ingredients together until well combined. Transfer into a small decorative serving dish. Refrigerate at least 1 hour to blend the flavors.

Sounds weird, but tastes great! A dandy appetizer dip—serve it with a rainbow of fresh, crisp vegetables.

Fresh Fruit Salsa

Makes about 3 cups (720 mL)

3 cups	peeled, finely chopped fruit (such as apples, pears, papaya, mangos, peaches or pineapple)	720 mL
½ – ⅔ cup	Salsa Fiesta! (page 145)	120 – 160 mL
½	lime, juice only	½
¼ cup	finely chopped coriander	60 mL

Stir all the ingredients together in a large mixing bowl. Cover and let stand at room temperature for at least half an hour before serving.

You can make a quick, fresh fruit salsa using homemade tomato salsa as a base. The contrasting flavors and textures of fruit salsa complement fried foods, like crab cakes, as well as grilled or barbecued meats or fish.

Blackberry, Rosemary and Red Wine Marinade

Makes about 1 cup (240 mL)

Absolutely fabulous with lamb. If you have fresh rosemary on hand, you can use a sprig as a brush to baste the meat while it is grilling.

½ cup	Blackberry Jam (page 33)	120 mL
¼ cup	red wine rosemary vinegar (page 181 to 183)	60 mL
¼ cup	red wine	60 mL
2 Tbsp.	grainy Dijon mustard	30 mL
2 Tbsp.	finely chopped fresh rosemary	30 mL

Sieve the blackberry jam to remove the seeds. In a small bowl, combine the jam with the remaining ingredients. Place lamb chops, kebabs or whatever you wish to marinate in a shallow pan and pour ⅔ of the marinade over top. Cover and refrigerate for at least 2 – 3 hours, or overnight. Use the reserved marinade to baste the meat during grilling.

Gingered Orange Spread

Makes about 1¼ cups (300 mL)

Perfect with Marmalade Oatmeal Muffins (page 211), English muffins or just plain toast.

1 cup	cream cheese, softened	240 mL
2 Tbsp.	orange juice	30 mL
3 Tbsp.	Traditional English Marmalade (page 70) or Orange Marmalade (page 71)	45 mL
2 tsp.	honey	10 mL
2 tsp.	chopped candied ginger or ½ tsp. (2.5 mL) ground ginger	10 mL
1 tsp.	finely grated orange zest	5 mL

Blend all the ingredients in a food processor for one minute. Place in a small crock or decorative serving dish. Chill until ready to use. Serve at room temperature.

Guacamole

Makes about 3 cups (720 mL)

Serve with salsa as a dip for tortilla chips or alongside any Mexican food.

4	large avocados, peeled and pitted	4
1/2	lime or small lemon, juice only	1/2
1/2 cup	finely chopped green bell peppers	120 mL
1/2 cup	finely chopped onion	120 mL
1/2 cup	finely chopped tomatoes	120 mL
1/4 cup	finely chopped celery	60 mL
1/4 cup	finely chopped cilantro	60 mL
3	cloves garlic, minced	3
3 Tbsp.	Salsa Fiesta! (page 145)	45 mL
1/2 tsp.	salt	2.5 mL
1/4 tsp.	freshly ground black pepper, or to taste	1.2 mL

Mash the avocados with a potato masher and squeeze the lime or lemon juice over top. Add the remaining ingredients and mix well. Transfer the guacamole to a serving dish. Cover with plastic wrap, pressing the plastic onto the surface of the guacamole. Refrigerate for at least 30 minutes before serving.

Fruit "Butters"

Jam or marmalade combined with softened butter makes a delightful spread for muffins, croissants, quick breads or waffles.

Cream 1/2 cup (120 mL) jam or marmalade and 1/3 cup (80 mL) butter together until smooth. Transfer the fruit butter to a small crock or decorative serving dish and chill until ready to serve. Serve at room temperature.

For a sweeter spread, add 1/2 tsp. (2.5 mL) sifted icing sugar. For a tarter spread, add 1/2 tsp. (2.5 mL) lemon juice or 2 tsp. (10 mL) finely grated orange zest. For a spicy spread, add 1/2 tsp. (2.5 mL) cinnamon or 2 tsp. (10 mL) finely chopped candied ginger.

Cumberland Sauce

Makes about 1½ cups (360 mL)

½ cup	ruby port	120 mL
½ cup	orange juice	120 mL
¼ cup	lemon juice	60 mL
1	shallot, minced	1
1 cup	Red Currant Jelly (page 61)	240 mL
2 tsp.	finely grated orange zest	10 mL
1 tsp.	finely grated lemon zest	5 mL
¼ tsp.	cayenne pepper	1.2 mL
¼ tsp.	ginger	1.2 mL

In a small pot, combine the port, orange juice and lemon juice. Bring to a boil over medium heat and simmer until reduced by half. Stir in the remaining ingredients and cook for another 15 minutes, until the mixture is slightly thickened. Remove from the heat. Let stand until cool, then refrigerate. Serve chilled.

Cumberland Sauce will keep for months in the refrigerator.

Cheddar Cheese Ball with Port and Dijon Mustard

Serves 12 to 16 as an appetizer

2	8-oz. (225-g) packages cream cheese, softened	2
3 cups	shredded aged Cheddar cheese	720 mL
¼ cup	port	60 mL
3 Tbsp.	very finely minced onion	45 mL
1 Tbsp.	Dijon mustard	15 mL
½ tsp.	paprika	2.5 mL
	parsley or chopped toasted walnuts or pecans	

Using a food processor, combine all the ingredients, except the nuts or parsley, until smooth. Refrigerate the mixture until it is firm enough to handle, about 1 hour. Shape into a ball. Wrap in plastic wrap and refrigerate at least 1 hour, or until ready to serve.

Remove from the refrigerator about 30 minutes before serving. Roll the ball in the chopped nuts or parsley to coat it. Place the cheese ball in the center of a platter and surround it with crackers. Pass the chutney.

Baked Brie with Chutney and Toasted Nuts

Serves 6 to 8 as an appetizer

1	4- to 5-inch (10- to 12.5-cm) whole Brie cheese	1
½ cup	chutney (pages 154 to 168)	120 mL
½ cup	coarsely chopped hazelnuts, walnuts or almonds	120 mL

Preheat the oven to 350°F (175°C). Unwrap the cheese and place it in a shallow, ovenproof dish. Bake the cheese for about 10 minutes. Spoon the chutney over the cheese, sprinkle with the nuts and bake for another 10 minutes, until the cheese is heated through, but not melted open. Remove from the oven and serve immediately.

An irresistible appetizer. Serve it with crackers, crusty bread, bagel chips or slices of red apples and green pears that have been tossed with lemon juice to prevent browning. You can use any chutney that you have on hand. Mango Chutney (page 154) and Pear Chutney (page 168) are favorites.

Chicken Breasts with Blueberries and Tarragon

Serves 4 to 6

Serve with buttered noodles or a mixture of brown and wild rice. Crisp green asparagus or snow peas make a lovely accompaniment.

2 Tbsp.	each olive oil and butter	30 mL
2	boneless skinless chicken breasts, halved	2
	salt and freshly ground black pepper to taste	
1/4 cup	flour	60 mL
1/2 cup	red wine	120 mL
1/4 cup	French Tarragon Vinegar (page 190)	60 mL
2/3 cup	chicken stock	160 mL
3 Tbsp.	finely chopped fresh tarragon	45 mL
1/2 cup	Blueberry Chutney (page 157)	120 mL
2/3 cup	cream	160 mL
1	egg yolk	1
2/3 cup	fresh blueberries	160 mL
	fresh tarragon sprigs	

Preheat the oven to 350°F (175°C).

In a large frying pan, heat the olive oil and butter until sizzling. Season the chicken with salt and pepper and cook for 2–3 minutes on each side to seal in the juices. Transfer the chicken to a greased, ovenproof casserole dish with a lid.

Stir the flour into the pan, scraping up any browned bits. Whisk in the wine, vinegar and chicken stock and bring to a boil. Stir in the tarragon and chutney. Pour the sauce over the chicken. Cover the casserole and bake for 30–40 minutes.

In a small bowl, whisk the cream and egg yolk together.

Remove the casserole from the oven. Remove the chicken breasts and set aside. Pour off about ½ cup (120 mL) liquid from the casserole dish and add it to the egg mixture. Mix well, then pour this mixture back into the casserole dish. Replace the chicken and add about ½ cup (120 mL) of the blueberries, reserving the rest for garnish. Cover and cook for another 10–15 minutes. Garnish with the remaining blueberries and the fresh tarragon.

Duck Breasts with Blackberry Cassis Sauce

Serves 4

4	duck breasts	4
	olive oil	
	salt and freshly ground black pepper to taste	
1 recipe	Blackberry Cassis Sauce	1 recipe

An impressive way to enjoy blackberries as an accompaniment to a main-course dish. The rich flavor of the duck is nicely balanced by the tartness of the berries.

Lightly brush the duck breasts with a little olive oil. Season with salt and pepper. Grill for 8–10 minutes on both sides. Remove to a serving plate. Spoon the warm Blackberry Cassis Sauce over the duck and serve immediately.

Blackberry Cassis Sauce

1 cup	Blackberry and Apple Chutney (page 167)	240 mL
½ cup	dry red wine	120 mL
2 cups	beef broth	475 mL
¼–½ cup	crème de cassis liqueur	60–120 mL
2 Tbsp.	butter	30 mL
1 cup	fresh blackberries	240 mL

Prepare the sauce before you grill the duck, and keep it warm.

Combine the chutney, red wine and beef broth. Bring to a boil over medium heat. Reduce the heat to medium-low and simmer gently until the mixture is reduced by half, stirring occasionally. Add the crème de cassis to taste. Just prior to serving, whisk in the butter and add the blackberries.

Old-Fashioned Glazed Baked Ham

Serves 8 to 10

1	5-lb. (2.25-kg) bone-in ham	1
1 recipe	Jelly Glaze, Marmalade Glaze, or Cranberry, Orange and Port Glaze (recipes below)	1 recipe

Preheat the oven to 350°F (175°C).

Remove the rind from the outside of the ham and trim the fat if necessary, leaving about a ¼-inch (.6-cm) layer to protect the meat. Score the fat in a diamond pattern, cutting only about ¼-inch (.6-cm) deep.

Place the ham, fat side up, on a wire rack in a shallow roasting pan. Bake the ham for 1 hour at 350°F (175°C). Remove from the oven. Increase the heat to 400°F (200°C). Spoon your choice of glaze over the ham. If desired, insert a whole clove in the center of each diamond. Bake another 15–20 minutes, basting often.

Jelly Glaze

In a small saucepan, heat 1 cup (240 mL) Red Currant Jelly (page 61) or Basic Apple Jelly (page 53) until melted.

Marmalade Glaze

1 cup	Traditional English Marmalade (page 70), Orange Marmalade (page 71), or Amber Marmalade (page 74)	240 mL
¼ cup	orange juice	60 mL
¼ cup	brown sugar	60 mL

Mix all ingredients together.

Cranberry, Orange and Port Glaze

¾ cup	Cranberry, Orange and Apricot Chutney (page 159)	180 mL
½ cup	brown sugar	120 mL
¼ cup	port	60 mL

Using a food processor or blender, purée the chutney until smooth. Blend in the sugar and port.

Marvellous Meat Loaf with Chili Sauce

Serves 6 to 8

A hearty mixture of ground beef, pork and vegetables spiked with your own homemade Chili Sauce. Not like Mom used to make!

1 cup	milk	240 mL
2 cups	soft breadcrumbs	475 mL
1 lb.	each ground beef and ground pork	454 g
½ cup	finely chopped onion	120 mL
½ cup	grated carrot	120 mL
¼ cup	chopped parsley	60 mL
1 cup	Country Style Chili Sauce, divided (page 172)	120 mL
2	eggs, well beaten	2
2 Tbsp.	prepared creamed horseradish or Dijon mustard	30 mL
2 tsp.	salt	10 mL
½ tsp.	freshly ground black pepper	2.5 mL

Preheat the oven to 350°F (175°C).

Combine the milk and breadcrumbs in a large bowl. Let stand for 5 minutes. Add the remaining ingredients, reserving ½ cup (120 mL) of the chili sauce. Mix thoroughly. Shape the mixture into a loaf and place on a lightly greased baking sheet. Spread the remaining ½ cup (120 mL) chili sauce over the top of the meat loaf. Bake for 1 hour.

Green Beans Mexicana

Serves 8

This versatile dish is equally good hot, cold or at room temperature.

2 lbs.	green beans, trimmed	900 g
2 Tbsp.	olive oil	30 mL
1 cup	Salsa Fiesta! (page 145)	240 mL
	salt and freshly ground black pepper to taste	
	fresh lemon juice	
1 Tbsp.	finely chopped fresh cilantro	15 mL

Bring a large pot of water to a boil and blanch the beans for 3–4 minutes. Do not overcook—they must be very crisp. Drain the beans in a colander, then plunge them into ice water to cool quickly. Drain again and blot them dry with paper towels.

Heat the olive oil in a large frying pan over high heat until it sizzles. Add the salsa and stir until hot, about 2 minutes. Add the beans and cook for about 5 minutes, until the beans are hot but still crisp. Season with salt and pepper. Squeeze a little lemon juice over (just a quick squeeze!). Transfer the beans to a serving platter and sprinkle with chopped cilantro.

Baked Banana Squash with Orange Marmalade

Serves 4 to 6

The tartness of the marmalade and the sweetness of the maple syrup give a wonderful complex flavor to the humble squash.

3 lbs.	banana squash	1.4 kg
	salt and freshly ground black pepper to taste	
¼ cup	Orange Marmalade (page 71)	60 mL
¼ cup	maple syrup	60 mL

Preheat the oven to 350°F (175°C).

Cut the squash into serving-size pieces and put it in an ungreased baking dish. Sprinkle with a little salt and pepper. Pour water into the dish to a depth of about ¼ inch (.6 cm). Cover the dish with foil and bake for about 30 minutes until the squash is tender.

Stir the marmalade and maple syrup together over medium-low heat until melted.

Remove the squash from the oven and drain. Spoon the marmalade-syrup mixture over the squash and bake for another 10–15 minutes.

Apple Glazed Carrots

Serves 4

2 cups	peeled, sliced carrots	475 mL
¼ cup	Apple Butter (page 110) or Honeyed Applesauce (page 104)	60 mL
3 Tbsp.	brown sugar	45 mL
2 Tbsp.	butter	30 mL

This is an easy dish to prepare when you are cooking a big dinner and don't have time to babysit your vegetables. It can easily be doubled or tripled.

Preheat the oven to 350°F (175°C).

Cook the carrots in boiling water until just tender. Drain and set aside.

In the same saucepan, heat the apple butter or applesauce, brown sugar and butter together until the sugar dissolves, about 5 minutes.

Place the carrots in a greased, shallow baking dish. Pour the apple mixture over the carrots. Bake for 15 minutes.

Rhubarb Ginger Chutney and Walnut Loaf

Makes 1 loaf

A favorite for breakfast, at tea-time or even as a simple dessert, this is terrific toasted.

2¼ cups	flour	535 mL
1 Tbsp.	baking powder	15 mL
½ tsp.	salt	2.5 mL
½ tsp.	cinnamon	2.5 mL
1 cup	chopped walnuts	240 mL
3 Tbsp.	butter, softened	45 mL
½ cup	honey	120 mL
3	eggs	3
1 cup	Rhubarb and Ginger Chutney (page 166)	240 mL

Preheat the oven to 350°F (175°C). Grease a 9 × 5 × 3-inch (23 × 13 × 7-cm) loaf pan.

In a small bowl, mix together the flour, baking powder, salt, cinnamon and walnuts. Set aside.

In a large bowl, cream the butter and honey until smooth. Beat in the eggs, one at a time. Stir in the chutney. Add the dry ingredients, stirring just until blended.

Turn into the prepared pan. Bake for 50 – 60 minutes. When done, the bread should be quite moist-looking, but will not be wet in the center. Cool on a rack. This bread is at its best when it is sliced and served the next day.

Marmalade Oatmeal Muffins

Makes 16 to 18 muffins

Serve with Gingered Orange Spread (page 200). These are best served warm.

2 cups	old-fashioned rolled oats	475 mL
2 cups	whole wheat flour	475 mL
5 tsp.	baking powder	25 mL
1 tsp.	salt	5 mL
1 cup	golden raisins	240 mL
½ cup	chopped walnuts	120 mL
2	eggs	2
¾ cup	Traditional English Marmalade (page 70), Orange Marmalade (page 71) or Amber Marmalade (page 74)	180 mL
½ cup	orange juice	120 mL
½ cup	vegetable oil	120 mL
1 cup	milk	240 mL
2 tsp.	finely grated orange peel	10 mL

Preheat the oven to 400°F (200°C). Grease the muffin tins.

In a large mixing bowl, stir together the rolled oats, flour, baking powder, salt, raisins and walnuts.

In a smaller bowl, beat the eggs lightly, then beat in the remaining ingredients. Make a well in the center of the dry ingredients. Pour in the egg mixture, stirring only enough to moisten the dry ingredients.

Spoon the batter into the greased muffin tins, filling them about ⅔ full. Bake for 20–25 minutes.

Applesauce Spice Cake with Cream Cheese Icing

Makes a 13 × 9-inch (33 × 23-cm) cake

2½ cups	flour	600 mL
2 cups	sugar	475 mL
1½ tsp.	baking soda	7.5 mL
1 tsp.	salt	5 mL
½ tsp.	baking powder	2.5 mL
1 tsp.	cinnamon	5 mL
½ tsp.	each cloves, nutmeg, ginger and cardamom	2.5 mL
2	eggs	2
1½ cups	Honeyed Applesauce (page 104)	360 mL
½ cup	water	120 mL
½ cup	shortening	120 mL
1 recipe	Cream Cheese Icing (below)	1 recipe

Preheat the oven to 350°F (175°C). Grease and flour one 13 × 9 × 2-inch (33 × 23 × 5-cm) oblong pan.

In a large mixing bowl, combine all the ingredients. Using an electric mixer, beat at low speed for about 1 minute, scraping the sides of the bowl often. Beat another 2 minutes at high speed, scraping the bowl occasionally.

Scrape the batter into the pan, spreading it evenly. Bake about 1 hour, or until a toothpick inserted in the center of the cake comes out clean. Cool on a rack. When it is completely cool, frost with Cream Cheese Icing.

Cream Cheese Icing

1 cup	cream cheese, softened	240 mL
1/2 cup	icing sugar	120 mL
1 Tbsp.	orange juice	15 mL
2 tsp.	finely grated orange zest	10 mL

In a small bowl, beat the cream cheese with an electric mixer on low speed. Gradually blend in the icing sugar with the orange juice and zest.

Apricot Coconut Drops

Makes about 36 cookies

1/2 cup	cream cheese, softened	120 mL
1/2 cup	butter, softened	120 mL
1/4 cup	sugar	60 mL
1/2 cup	Apricot Jam (page 37)	120 mL
1/4 tsp.	almond extract	1.2 mL
1 1/2 cups	flour	360 mL
1 1/2 tsp.	baking powder	7.5 mL
1/4 tsp.	salt	1.2 mL
1/2 cup	flaked coconut	120 mL

These cookies are quick and easy to make. Check the cookies while baking to ensure that they are not getting overdone on the bottom, especially if you're using a dark-colored cookie sheet.

Preheat the oven to 350°F (175°C).

In a large bowl, beat the cream cheese, butter and sugar with an electric mixer until combined. Mix in the jam and almond extract. Stir in the remaining ingredients until well mixed.

Using a teaspoon, drop small spoonfuls of the dough onto a cookie sheet, spacing them 2 inches (5 cm) apart.

Bake for 15–20 minutes until lightly browned. Remove from the cookie sheet and cool on wire racks.

Lemon Cheesecake

Serves 12 to 14

Serve this elegant, subtly flavored cheesecake with Blackberry Orange Sauce with Port (page 101), Honeyed Peach and Blueberry Compote (page 100), Pineapple, Strawberry and Rhubarb Dessert Sauce (page 99) or Spirited Cherry and Raspberry Compote (page 102).

Crust:

1¾ cups	finely crushed graham wafer crumbs	420 mL
¼ cup	very finely chopped walnuts	60 mL
½ cup	melted butter	120 mL
2 Tbsp.	sugar	30 mL

Preheat the oven to 350°F (175°C). Mix all the ingredients together until crumbly. Press the crumbs into the bottom and up about ⅔ of the sides of a 9-inch (23-cm) springform pan. Bake for 10 minutes. Set aside while you make the filling.

Filling:

1 lb.	cream cheese, softened	450 g
¾ cup	sugar	180 mL
3	eggs	3
½ cup	sour cream	120 mL
2 Tbsp.	lemon juice	30 mL
2 tsp.	finely grated lemon zest	10 mL

Beat the cream cheese until it is light and fluffy, using an electric mixer. Gradually beat in the sugar. Beat in the eggs one at a time. Scrape down the sides of the bowl occasionally. Mix in the sour cream, lemon juice and zest.

Pour the mixture over the crust. Bake at 350°F (175°C) for 40–45 minutes, or until set. Remove from the oven.

Topping:

1 cup	sour cream	240 mL
1/4 cup	sugar	60 mL
2 Tbsp.	lemon juice	30 mL

Mix the sour cream, sugar and lemon juice together. Spread over the hot cheesecake. Return to the oven to bake for an additional 10 minutes.

Remove the cheesecake from the oven. Cool for 30 minutes. Loosen the sides of the springform pan, but leave them in place. When the cheesecake has cooled thoroughly, refrigerate it for at least 6 hours, preferably overnight.

Remove the cake from the pan. Transfer it to a serving platter. To serve, spoon over any of your homemade fruit sauces or preserves. You may also use any jam or conserve thinned to spreading consistency (if necessary) with a little fruit juice, fruit liqueur or brandy.

Use any flavor of jam,
marmalade or conserve
to make this cookie.
Just be sure to choose
one that is rather thick.

Jim Jams

Makes about 30 to 36 cookies

1 cup	jam of your choice (pages 32 to 44)	240 mL
½ cup	raisins, chopped	120 mL
½ cup	chopped pecans	120 mL
1 cup	butter	240 mL
1 cup	brown sugar	240 mL
2	eggs	2
2 cups	flour	475 mL
2 tsp.	baking powder	10 mL
½ tsp.	salt	2.5 mL
1 tsp.	cinnamon	5 mL
½ tsp.	cloves	2.5 mL
½ cup	milk	120 mL
2 cups	oatmeal	475 mL

Preheat the oven to 350°F (175°C).

Mix together the jam, raisins and pecans. Set aside.

In a large bowl, cream the butter and sugar until fluffy. Beat in the eggs.

In a third bowl, combine the flour, baking powder, salt, cinnamon and cloves. Add the dry mixture alternately with the milk to the creamed mixture. Stir in the oatmeal.

Reserve about ¾ cup (180 mL) of the dough.

Drop the remainder of the dough by teaspoonfuls onto a greased cookie sheet, spacing them about 2 inches (5 cm) apart. Make an indentation in the center of each cookie, spoon in a little of the jam mixture, then place a dab of reserved dough on top.

Bake for 10–15 minutes. Remove from the cookie sheet and cool on wire racks.

Gifts from
the Pantry

*The art of giving presents is to give something which others
cannot buy for themselves.*

—A . A. Milne

Like cooking for the ones you love, giving gifts to family and
friends is one of life's simple pleasures. This is especially true
when they are gifts that you have made yourself.

At harvest time, in the midst of the busiest preserving season of all, it is easy to forget that another, even busier season is
just around the corner. When our kitchens are full of steam
and we are up to our elbows in peaches or tomatoes, visions of
sugar plums couldn't be further from our minds.

But be assured, Christmas is closer than you think. And so
are a host of other eagerly anticipated or totally unexpected
occasions that will require giving a gift of one kind of another.

The farsighted home preserver has it made—literally. Like
an industrious squirrel hiding away a supply of nuts for the
winter, the prudent home preserver will prepare extra jars
of favorite condiments for the gift-giving season that looms
so near.

If you make a little extra, here and there, when fruits
and vegetables are in season, you can stockpile an impressive
supply of food to give as gifts for any occasion throughout
the year.

Virtually everyone appreciates a gift of good food, and
homemade preserves have a universal appeal. They can even be
tailor-made to suit the individual preferences of the recipient, if
you know their tastes.

When you give preserves as gifts, you are giving a gift of
your time and creativity. The hours you spend making homemade preserves cannot be duplicated by simply running out
and picking something up from a store. The thoughtfulness of
a homemade gift makes the recipient feel very special.

Preserves are ideal to take along to any social gathering when a little token for the host or hostess would be appropriate. A beautifully presented bottle of infused vinegar can be a worthy substitute for the customary bottle of wine, especially if your hosts do not drink alcohol. A tangy jar of pickled beans would be a hit at a cocktail party, a savory relish or chutney perfect for an invitation to a barbecue. And, of course, a fruity jam or jelly is just the thing for a brunch or an afternoon tea.

I almost hate to mention it, but giving preserves as gifts can be very economical too. Last-minute gifts almost always cost more money, since we don't have the time to shop shrewdly. With a good selection of preserves on hand, you will have delicious, useful gifts appropriate for practically anyone — and they will cost pennies instead of the earth.

There is an old saying that "the man who chops his own wood warms himself twice." And you will feel the warmth of pride and satisfaction twice if you give homemade gifts from your pantry — once in the making and once again in the giving.

Packaging and Presentation

Part of the joy of giving is the originality and creativity of the packaging. Since your gift is already made, you can spend a little extra time on the finishing touches that will make it truly one of a kind.

Any present can be enhanced by its wrapping. An attractively wrapped gift is a feast for the eyes.

Packaging and presentation involves a little planning ahead on your part. Always be on the lookout for items that might serve as attractive containers in which to present your preserves. Save and recycle pretty boxes, tins, paper and bags. You can wrap or cover uninteresting containers with fabric or beautiful paper. Some containers lend themselves to being painted. Save baskets of all shapes and sizes. An assortment of preserves can be a visually striking gift. An antique soup tureen from a garage sale (or your attic), a terracotta pot from the florist, a charming wicker basket from Chinatown — any of these can attractively display a selection of preserves. Just wrap it with cellophane and add a festive bow. Kitchenware, either new or vintage, can double as interesting containers to hold just one or several jars of preserves. Try a colander, a handmade pottery bowl, a delicate china cup and saucer, a wok or an Oriental bamboo steamer.

Check out thrift stores, rummage sales or garage sales for unusual jars or elegant decanters. You may even find antique canning jars, old-fashioned bail-type jars (glass-lidded jars with curved wire fasteners) or hinged, clamp-type jars from Europe. Preserves can be transferred to these decorative containers as long as the container is thoroughly washed and sterilized first, but once transferred, the foods must be kept refrigerated. If you choose to give preserves packaged in containers that have not been heat-sealed, make sure to include instructions for refrigerator storage with your gift. Small jars and bottles can also be purchased from cookware shops, hardware stores, even discount and dollar stores.

Give your bottles and jars an expensive "gourmet shop" look by adding inexpensive decorative touches. Everyone has seen pretty jars of jam or jelly done up with little paper or fabric "hats," or lid covers, secured with a bow. This is very easy to do.

Covers can be made from many different types of fabric. Make sure the fabric is not too heavy, stiff or bulky to smoothly fit over the top of the jar. The best choices are cottons or cotton blends. Choose a fabric that doesn't fray too much and that can be cut easily with pinking shears. Avoid thin, sheer or see-through fabrics unless you want to double them. Small-scale prints are best, in keeping with the size of the jar.

Paper can also be used successfully. It should be pliable enough to go over the jar, but not so thin that it will tear. Brown paper, gift wrap, some wallpapers and other similar-weight papers are appropriate. Tissue paper is not. A neat craft product called "paper twist" can be unravelled and cut to fit.

To make lid covers, measure the top of your jar and add about 3½ inches (10 cm) for a nice frill. Now find a small plate or lid or anything round that is approximately that size to use as a template. (I find that a side plate is the perfect size to cover a standard-sized preserving jar lid, while one of my salad plates fits the wide-mouthed lid to a T.)

Using the plate as a guide, draw as many circles as you need to cover your jars. If you are using fabric, use pinking shears to cut the circles so the fabric will not fray. For paper, use the shears for a decorative edge or regular scissors for a plain one.

You can affix the fabric or paper to the jar lid using a glue gun or white craft glue, or you can simply center the decorative top on the lid and secure it around the neck of the jar with an elastic band. If you are using paper, be extra careful to avoid tearing it. Sometimes you need to do a little adjusting at the neck to get the proper ruffled effect.

Tie a bow around the neck of the jar to decorate it and to hide the elastic band. You can use a matching or contrasting ribbon, raffia, jute twine, string, thick strands of wool — whatever works for you.

Fabric stores have wonderful materials printed with fruits and vegetables that are really fun. At Christmas, you can use seasonal fabrics with Santas or snowmen and decorate them with glued-on pine cones or holly.

Other decorative accessories can be glued on as well. Bits of dried flowers, seed pods, whole spices such as cinnamon sticks or star anise, dried chili peppers or dried orange or apple slices are good ideas. But don't overdo it. Too much will detract from the overall presentation.

Another attractive look is to swathe bottles of vinegar or jars with white tissue, gauze or tulle, secure around the neck with French wired ribbon, then tie on a single full-blown artificial rose. (A nice one, not a cheap one.) Red fruit vinegars look festive with clumps of imitation berries or greenery tied at the neck with a flowing ribbon or raffia.

A bright strip of grosgrain ribbon firmly fastened with sealing wax adds a professional touch to gifts. Sealing wax sticks and decorative metal seals are available at many craft stores and specialty stationery shops. All you have to do is wrap the ribbon around the jar and anchor it in place temporarily, using masking tape. Light the stick of sealing wax following the package directions and hold it about 1 inch (2.5 cm) above the spot to be sealed. Allow the wax to drip continuously until you have a blob about 1 inch (2.5 cm) in diameter. Press the metal seal down firmly onto the melted wax. Wait a couple of seconds before lifting the seal to ensure that a clear impression has been made. Remove the masking tape. You might like to practice the technique a little before you try it on your jars of preserves, just to be sure that you've got the hang of it.

A really beautiful look for extra-special gifts is to cover the jar lids with leaves that have been soaked in glycerine. Glycerine, available at most drugstores, preserves the leaves, keeping them moist and supple.

Wash and dry large leaves, such as maple, and brush both sides with the glycerine. Place the leaves over the top of the jar, overlapping them slightly if necessary. Wrap the lid in plastic wrap and fasten with an elastic band. Place a weight on top and refrigerate overnight. Carefully unwrap the jar and blot up any excess glycerine. Tie a length of raffia around the neck of the jar and finish with a bow.

A gift of food can be as simple as a prettily decorated jar of jam or as elaborate as an elegant basket chock-full of vinegars and exotic condiments.

The most appreciated gifts are often those that people took the time and the effort to make themselves. Spend just a bit more time and make your gifts of home preserves even more special.

Labels and Tags

Most brands of preserving jars have adhesive-backed labels included in the package, but if you are recycling jars, you won't have this option. And while adequate for identification purposes, these labels are rather ordinary — you can produce more attractive, unusual labels with a little time and effort.

Packaged labels with appealing designs especially made for preserving jars are available and often come preprinted with "Contents" or "From the Kitchen of ... " These can usually be found at cookbook or cookware stores and some stationery shops.

Office supply stores are a good source for plain, gummed mailing labels. These can be dressed up with pretty fruit and vegetable stickers or stamps. Some stores carry unique labels with old-fashioned drawings.

Tie-on tags can be elegant or rustic looking. Gift enclosure cards make good tags; cut-up Christmas cards or trimmed-down cards from birthdays or other special occasions also work well. You can even buy special scissors to give these tags a scalloped or decorative edge.

Beautiful tags can be made by covering one side of heavy cardstock with gift wrap, adhesive-backed paper or fabric.

To attach the tags, punch a hole in one corner using a paper punch, then thread raffia, ribbon or whatever you like through the hole and around the neck of the jar.

Use plain brown baggage tags or heavy brown paper for a rustic, country look. And, of course, you can print labels or tags using your home computer. Don't go for anything too high-tech—you want a simple design to complement your preserves.

Enclose serving suggestions or recipes with your gifts of homemade preserves, so that your friends will know how to use them. And don't forget to note that refrigerator storage is required for all preserves (except vinegar) once they have been opened.

Index

About the Author

Born in Vancouver, British Columbia, but raised in eastern Canada, Mary Anne Dragan has always had a keen interest in cooking. At an early age, she was baking for the local fall fair and selling birthday cakes to friends and neighbors.

Mary Anne originally pursued a career in cooking, but is now employed in the "front end" of the hospitality business at one of Vancouver's finest restaurants. She also owns and runs Well Preserved, a seasonal business selling jams, pickles and chutneys. This is her first cookbook.